THE COELUM PHILOSOPHORUM

or

THE BOOK OF VEXATIONS

THE COELUM PHILOSOPHORUM,

or

THE BOOK OF VEXATIONS

PHILIPPUS THEOPHRASTUS PARACELSUS.

THE SCIENCE AND NATURE OF ALCHEMY, AND WHAT
OPINION SHOULD BE
FORMED THEREOF.
Regulated by the Seven Rules or Fundamental Canons
according to the seven commonly known Metals

Table of Contents

The Preface

The Seven Canons of the Metals

Concerning the Tincture of the Philosophers

The Treasure of Treasures for Alchemists.

The Aurora of the Philosophers

A Short Catechism of Alchemy

The Alchemist, Duke University

Testamentum Johannis Dee Philosophi Summi ad Johannem Gwynn

This Letter third and last I minde to make,
At your request for very vertues sake;
Your written panges, and methods set aside,
From that I byd, looke that you never slide.
Cut that in Three, which Nature hath made One,
Then strengthen hyt, even by it self alone,
Wherewith then Cutte the poudred Sonne in twayne,
By length of tyme, and heale the woonde againe.
The self same Sunne twys yet more, ye must wounde,
Still with new Knives, of the same kinde, and grounde;
Our Monas trewe thus use by natures Law,
Both binde and lewse, only with rype and rawe,
And ay thanke God who only is our Guyde,
All is ynugh, no more then at this Tyde.

1568

THE PREFACE
OF THEOPHRASTUS PARACELSUS TO ALL ALCHEMISTS AND READERS
OF THIS BOOK.

You who are skilled in Alchemy, and as many others as promise yourselves great riches or chiefly desire to make gold and silver, which Alchemy in different ways promises and teaches; equally, too, you who willingly undergo toil and vexations, and wish not to be freed from them, until you have attained your rewards, and the fulfilment of the promises made to you; experience teaches this every day, that out of thousands of you not even one accomplishes his desire. Is this a failure of Nature or of Art? I say, no; but it is rather the fault of fate, or of the unskilfulness of the operator.

Since, therefore, the characters of the sign of the stars and planets of heaven, together with the other names, inverted words, receipts, materials, and instruments are thoroughly well known to such as are acquainted with this art, it would be altogether superfluous to recur to these same subjects in the present book, although the use of such signs, names, and characters at the proper time is by no means without advantage.

But herein will be noticed another way of treating Alchemy different from the previous method, and deduced by Seven Canons from the sevenfold series of the metals. This, indeed, will not give scope for a pompous parade of words, but, nevertheless, in the consideration of those Canons everything which should be separated from Alchemy will be treated at sufficient length, and, moreover, many secrets of other things are herein contained.

Hence, too, result certain marvellous speculations and new operations which frequently differ from the writings and opinions of ancient operators and natural philosophers, but have been discovered and confirmed by full proof and experimentation.

Moreover, in this Art nothing is more true than this, though it be little known and gains small confidence. All the fault and cause of difficulty in Alchemy, whereby very many persons are reduced to poverty, and others labour in vain, is wholly and solely lack of skill in the operator, and the defect or excess of materials, whether in quantity or quality, whence it ensues that, in the course of operation, things are wasted or reduced to nothing. If the true process shall have been found, the substance itself while transmuting approaches daily more and more towards perfection. The straight road is easy, but it is found by very few.

Sometimes it may happen that a speculative artist may, by his own eccentricity, think out for himself some new method in Alchemy, be the consequence anything or nothing. He need do nought in order to reduce something into nothing, and again bring back something out of nothing. Yet this proverb of the incredulous is not wholly false. Destruction perfects that which is good; for the good cannot appear on account of that which conceals it. The good is least good whilst it is thus concealed. The concealment must be removed that so the good may be able freely to appear in its own brightness. For example, the mountain, the sand, the earth, or the stone in which a metal has grown is such a concealment. Each one of the visible metals is a concealment of the other six metals.

By the element of fire all that is imperfect is destroyed and taken away, as, for instance, the five metals, Mercury, Jupiter, Mars, Venus, and Saturn.[1] On the other hand, the perfect metals, Sol and Luna, are not consumed in that same fire. They remain in the fire: and at the same time, out of the other imperfect ones which are destroyed, they assume their own body and become visible to the eyes. How, and by what method, this comes about can be gathered from the Seven Canons. Hence it may be learnt what are the nature and property of each metal, what it effects with the other metals, and what are its powers in commixture with them.

But this should be noted in the very first place: that these Seven Canons cannot be perfectly understood by every cursory reader at a first glance or a single reading. An inferior intelligence does not easily perceive occult and abstruse subjects. Each one of these Canons demands no slight discussion. Many persons, puffed up with pride, fancy they can easily comprehend all which this book comprises. Thus they set down its contents as useless and futile, thinking they have something far better of their own, and that therefore they can afford to despise what is here contained.

THE SEVEN CANONS OF THE METALS.

THE FIRST CANON.
CONCERNING THE NATURE AND PROPERTIES OF MERCURY.[2]

All things are concealed in all. One of them all is the concealer of the rest – their corporeal vessel, external, visible, and movable. All liquefactions are manifested in that vessel. For the vessel is a living and corporeal spirit, and so all coagulations or congelations enclosed in it, when prevented from flowing and surrounded, are not therewith content. No name can be found for this liquefaction, by which it may be designated; still less can it be found for its origin. And since no heat is so strong as to be equalised therewith, it should be compared to the fire of Gehenna. A liquefaction of this kind has no sort of connection with others made by the heat of natural fire, or congelated or coagulated by natural cold. These congelations, through their weakness, are unable to obtain in Mercury, and therefore, on that account, he altogether contemns them. Hence one may gather that elementary powers, in their process of destruction, can add nothing to, nor take away anything from, celestial powers (which are called Quintessence or its elements), nor have they any capacity for operating. Celestial and infernal powers do not obey the four elements, whether they be dry, moist, hot, or cold. No one of them has the faculty of acting against a Quintessence; but each one contains within itself its own powers and means of action.[3]

THE SECOND CANON.
CONCERNING THE NATURE AND PROPERTIES OF JUPITER.

In that which is manifest (that is to say, the body of Jupiter) the other six corporeal metals are spiritually concealed, but one more deeply and more tenaciously than another. Jupiter has nothing of a Quintessence in his composition, but is of the nature of the four elementaries. On this account this liquefaction is brought about by the application of a moderate fire, and, in like manner, he is coagulated by moderate cold. He has affinity with the liquefactions of all the other metals. For the more like he is to some other nature, the more easily he is united thereto by conjunction. For the operation of those nearly allied is easier and more natural than of those which are remote. The remote body does not press upon the other. At the same time, it is not feared, though it may be very powerful. Hence it happens that men do not aspire to the superior orders of creation, because they are far distant from them, and do not see their glory. In like manner, they do not much fear those of an inferior order, because they are remote, and none of the living knows their condition or has experienced the misery of their punishment. For this cause an infernal spirit is accounted as nothing. For more remote objects are on that account held more cheaply and occupy a lower place, since according to the propriety of its position each object turns out better, or is transmuted. This can be proved by various examples.

The more remote, therefore, Jupiter is found to be from Mars and Venus, and the nearer Sol and Luna, the more "goldness" or "silveriness", if I may so say, it contains in its body, and the greater, stronger, more visible, more tangible, more amiable, more acceptable, more distinguished, and more true it is found than in some remote body. Again, the more remote a thing is, of the less account is it esteemed in all the respects aforesaid, since what is present is always preferred before what is absent. In proportion as the nearer is clear the more remote is occult. This, therefore, is a point which you, as an Alchemist, must seriou(S)ly debate with yourself, how you can relegate Jupiter to a remote and abstruse place, which Sol and Luna occupy, and how, in turn, you can summon Sol and Luna from remote positions to a near place, where Jupiter is corporeally posited; so that, in the same way, Sol and Luna also may really be present there corporeally before your eyes. For the transmutation of metals from imperfection to perfection there are several practical receipts. Mix the one with the other. Then again separate the one pure from the other. This is nothing else but the process of permutation, set in order by perfect alchemical labour. Note that Jupiter has much gold and not a little silver. Let Saturn and Luna be imposed on him, and of the rest Luna will be augmented.[4]

THE THIRD CANON.
CONCERNING MARS AND HIS PROPERTIES.

The six occult metals have expelled the seventh from them, and have made it corporeal, leaving it little efficacy, and imposing on it great hardness and weight. This being the case, they have shaken off all their own strength of coagulation and hardness, which they manifest in this other body. On the contrary, they have retained in themselves their colour and liquefaction, together with their nobility. It is very difficult and laborious for a prince or a king to be produced out of an unfit and common man. But Mars acquires dominion. with strong and pugnacious hand, and seizes on the position of king. He should, however, be on his guard against snares; that he be not led captive suddenly and unexpectedly. It must also be considered by what method Mars may be able to take the place of king, and Sol and Luna, with Saturn, hold the place of Mars.[5]

THE FOURTH CANON.
CONCERNING VENUS AND ITS PROPERTIES.

The other six metals have rendered Venus an extrinsical body by means of all their colour and method of liquefaction. It may be necessary, in order to understand this, that we should show, by some examples, how a manifest thing may be rendered occult, and an occult thing rendered materially manifest by means of fire. Whatever is combustible can be naturally transmuted by fire from one form into another, namely, into lime, soot, ashes, glass, colours, stones, and earth. This last can again be reduced to many new metallic bodies. If a metal, too, be burnt, or rendered fragile by old rust, it can again acquire malleability by applications of fire.[6]

THE FIFTH CANON.
CONCERNING THE NATURE AND PROPERTIES OP SATURN.

Of his own nature Saturn speaks thus: The other six have cast me out as their examiner. They have thrust me forth from them and from a spiritual place. They have also added a corruptible body as a place of abode, so that I may be what they neither are nor desire to become. My six brothers are spiritual, and thence it ensues that so often as I am put in the fire they penetrate my body and, together with me, perish in the fire, Sol and Luna excepted. These are purified and ennobled in my water. My spirit is a water softening the rigid and congealed bodies of my brothers. Yet my body is inclined to the earth. Whatever is received into me becomes conformed thereto, and by means of us is converted into one body. It would be of little use to the world if it should learn, or at least believe, what lies hid in me, and what I am able to effect. It would be more profitable it should ascertain what I am able to do with myself. Deserting all the methods of the Alchemists, it would then use only that which is in me and can be done by me. The stone of cold is in me. This is a water by means of which I make the spirits of the six metals congeal into the essence of the seventh, and this is to promote Sol with Luna.[7]

Two kinds of Antimony are found: one the common black by which Sol is purified when liquefied therein. This has the closest affinity with Saturn. The other kind is the white, which is also called Magnesia and Bismuth. It has great affinity with Jupiter, and when mixed with the other Antimony it augments Luna.

THE SIXTH CANON.
CONCERNING LUNA AND THE PROPERTIES THEREOF.

The endeavour to make Saturn or Mars out of Luna involves no lighter or easier work than to make Luna, with great gain, out of Mercury, Jupiter, Mars, Venus, or Saturn. It is not useful to transmute what is perfect into what is imperfect, but the latter into the former. Nevertheless, it is well to know what is the material of Luna, or whence it proceeds. Whoever is not able to consider or find this out will neither be able to make Luna. It will be asked, What is Luna? It is among the seven metals which are spiritually concealed, itself the seventh, external, corporeal, and material. For this seventh always contains the six metals spiritually hidden in itself. And the six spiritual metals do not exist without one external and material metal. So also no corporeal metal can have place or essence without those six spiritual ones. The seven corporeal metals mix easily by means of liquefaction, but this mixture is not useful for making Sol or Luna. For in that mixture each metal remains in its own nature, or fixed in the fire, or flies from it. For example, mix, in any way you can, Mercury, Jupiter, Saturn, Mars, Venus, Sol, and Luna. It will not thence result that Sol and Luna will so change the other five that, by the agency of Sol and Luna, these will become Sol and Luna. For though all be liquefied into a single mass, nevertheless each remains in its nature whatever it is. This is the judgment which must be passed on corporeal mixture. But concerning spiritual mixture and communion of the metals, it should be known that no separation or mortification is spiritual, because such spirits can never exist without bodies. Though the body should be taken away from them and mortified a hundred times in one hour, nevertheless, they would always acquire another much more noble than the former. And this is the transposition of the metals from one death to another, that is to say, from a lesser degree into one greater and higher, namely, into Luna; and from a better into the best and most most perfect, that is, into Sol, the brilliant and altogether royal metal. It is most true, then, as frequently said above, that the six metals always generate a seventh, or produce it from themselves clear in its *esse*.

A question may arise: If it be true that Luna and every metal derives its origin and is generated from the other six, what is then its property and its nature? To this we reply: From Saturn, Mercury, Jupiter, Mars, Venus, and Sol, nothing and no other metal than Luna could be made. The cause is that each metal has two good virtues of the other six, of which altogether there are twelve. These are the spirit of Luna, which thus in a few words may be made known. Luna is composed of the six spiritual metals and their virtues, whereof each possesses two. Altogether, therefore, twelve are thus posited in one corporeal metal, which are compared to the seven planets and the twelve celestial signs. Luna has from the planet Mercury, and from Aquarius and Pisces, its liquidity and bright white colour. So Luna has from Jupiter, with Sagittarius and Taurus, its white colour and its great firmness in fire. Luna has from Mars, with Cancer and Aries, its hardness and its clear sound. Luna has from Venus, with Gemini and Libra, its measure of coagulation and its From Saturn, with Virgo and Scorpio, its homogeneous body, with gravity. From Sol, with Leo and Virgo, its spotless purity and great constancy against the power of fire. Such is the knowledge of the natural exaltation and of the course of the spirit and body of Luna, with its composite nature and wisdom briefly summarised. Furthermore, it should be pointed out what kind of a body such metallic spirits acquire in their primitive generation by means of celestial influx. For the metal-digger, when he has crushed the stone, contemptible as it is in appearance, liquefies it, corrupts it, and altogether mortifies it with fire. Then this metallic spirit, in such a process of mortification, receives a better and more noble body, not friable but malleable. Then comes the Alchemist, who again corrupts, mortifies, and artificially prepares such a metallic body. Thus once more that spirit of the metal assumes a more noble and more perfect body, putting itself forward clearly into the light, except it be Sol or Luna. Then at last the metallic spirit and body are perfectly united, are safe from the corruption of elementary fire, and also incorruptible.[8]

THE SEVENTH CANON.
CONCERNING THE NATURE OF SOL AND ITS PROPERTIES.

The seventh after the six spiritual metals is corporeally Sol, which in itself is nothing but pure fire. What in outward appearance is more beautiful, more brilliant, more clear and perceptible, a heavier, colder, or more homogeneous body to see? And it is easy to perceive the cause of this, namely, that it contains in itself the congelations of the other six metals, out of which it is made externally into one most compact body. Its liquefaction proceeds from elementary fire, or is caused by the liquations of Mercury, with Pisces and Aquarius, concealed spiritually within it. The most manifest proof of this is that Mercury is easily mingled corporeally with the Sun as in an embrace. But for Sol, when the heat is withdrawn and the cold supervenes after liquefaction, to coagulate and to become hard and solid, there is need of the other five metals, whose nature it embraces in itself – Jupiter, Saturn, Mars, Venus, Luna. In these five metals the cold abodes with their regimens are especially found. Hence it happens that Sol can with difficulty be liquefied without the heat of fire, on account of the cold whereof mention has been made. For Mercury cannot assist with his natural heat or liquefaction, or defend himself against the cold of the five metals, because the heat of Mercury is not sufficient to retain Sol in a state of liquefaction. Wherefore Sol has to obey the five metals rather than Mercury alone. Mercury itself has no office of itself save always to flow. Hence it happens that in coagulations of the other metals it can effect nothing, since its nature is not to make anything hard or solid, but liquid. To render fluid is the nature of heat and life, but cold has the nature of hardness, consolidation, and immobility, which is compared to death. For example, the six cold metals, Jupiter, Venus, Saturn, Mars, Venus, Luna, if they are to be liquefied must be brought to that condition by the heat of fire. Snow or ice, which are cold, will not produce this effect, but rather will harden. As soon as ever the metal liquefied by fire is removed therefrom, the cold, seizing upon it, renders it hard, congelated, and immovable of itself. But in order that Mercury may remain fluid and alive continually, say, I pray you, whether this will be affected with heat on cold? Whoever answers that this is brought about by a cold and damp nature, and that it has its life from cold – the promulgator of this opinion, having no knowledge of Nature, is led away by the vulgar. For the vulgar man judges only falsely, and always holds firmly on to his error. So then let him who loves truth withdraw therefrom. Mercury, in fact, lives not at all from cold but from a warm and fiery nature. Whatever lives is fire, because heat is life, but cold the occasion of death. The fire of Sol is of itself pure, not indeed alive, but hard, and so far shews the colour of sulphur in that yellow and red are mixed therein in due proportion. The five cold metals are Jupiter, Mars, Saturn, Venus, and Luna, which assign to Sol their virtues; according to cold, the body itself; according to fire, colour; according to dryness, solidity; according to humidity, weight; and out of brightness, sound. But that gold is not burned in the element of terrestrial fire, nor is even corrupted, is effected by the firmness of Sol. For one fire cannot burn another, or even consume it; but rather if fire be added to fire it is increased, and becomes more powerful in its operations. The celestial fire which flows to us on the earth from the Sun is not such a fire as there is in heaven, neither is it like that which exists upon the earth, but that celestial fire with us is cold and congealed, and it is the body of the Sun. Wherefore the Sun can in no way be overcome by our fire. This only happens, that it is liquefied, like snow or ice, by that same celestial Sun. Fire, therefore, has not the power of burning fire, because the Sun is fire, which, dissolved in heaven, is coagulated with us.

	1. Celestial	Dissolved
Gold is in its Essence threefold:	2. Elementary	And Fluid
	3. Metallic	Is Corporeal

THE END OF THE SEVEN CANONS.

CERTAIN TREATISES AND APPENDICES ARISING OUT OF THE SEVEN CANONS.

GOD AND NATURE DO NOTHING IN VAIN.

The eternal position of all things, independent of time, without beginning or end, operates everywhere. It works essentially where otherwise there is no hope. It accomplishes that which is deemed impossible. What appears beyond belief or hope emerges into truth after a wonderful fashion.

NOTE ON MERCURIUS VIVUS.

Whatever tinges with a white colour has the nature of life, and the properties and power of light, which causally produces life. Whatever, on the other hand, tinges with blackness, or produces black, has a nature in common with death, the properties of darkness, and forces productive of death. The earth with its frigidity is a coagulation and fixation of this kind of hardness. For the house is always dead; but he who inhabits the house lives. If you can discover the force of this illustration you have conquered.

Tested liquefactive powder.
Burn fat verbena.[9]

Recipe. – Salt nitre, four ounces; a moiety of sulphur; tartar, one ounce. Mix and liquefy.

WHAT IS TO BE THOUGHT CONCERNING THE CONGELATION OF MERCURY.

To mortify or congeal Mercury, and afterwards seek to turn it into Luna, and to sublimate it with great labour, is labour in vain, since it involves a dissipation of Sol and Luna existing therein. There is another method, far different and much more concise, whereby, with little waste of Mercury and less expenditure of toil, it is transmuted into Luna without congelation. Any one can at pleasure learn this Art in Alchemy, since it is so simple and easy; and by it, in a short time, he could make any quantity of silver and gold. It is tedious to read long descriptions, and everybody wishes to be advised in straightforward words. Do this, then; proceed as follows, and you will have Sol and Luna, by help whereof you will turn out a very rich man. Wait awhile, I beg, while this process is described to you in few words, and keep these words well digested, so that out of Saturn, Mercury, and Jupiter you may make Sol and Luna. There is not, nor ever will be, any art so easy to find out and practise, and so effective in itself. The method of making Sol and Luna by Alchemy is so prompt that there is no more need of books, or of elaborate instruction, than there would be if one wished to write about last year's snow.

CONCERNING THE RECEIPTS OF ALCHEMY.

What, then, shall we say about the receipts of Alchemy, and about the diversity of its vessels and instruments? These are furnaces, glasses, jars, waters, oils, limes, sulphurs, salts, saltpetres, alums, vitriols, chrysocollae, copper-greens, atraments, auri-pigments, fel vitri, ceruse, red earth, thucia, wax, lutum sapientiae, pounded glass, verdigris, soot, testae ovorum, crocus of Mars, soap, crystal, chalk, arsenic, antimony, minium, elixir, lazurium, gold-leaf, salt-nitre, sal ammoniac, calamine stone, magnesia, bolus armenus, and many other things. Moreover, concerning preparations, putrefactions, digestions, probations, solutions, cementings, filtrations, reverberations, calcinations, graduations, rectifications, amalgamations, purgations, etc., with these alchemical books are crammed. Then, again, concerning herbs, roots, seeds, woods, stones, animals, worms, bone dust, snail shells, other shells, and pitch. These and the like, whereof there are some very far-fetched in Alchemy, are mere incumbrances of work; since even if Sol and Luna could be made by them they rather hinder and delay than further one's purpose. But it is not from these – to say the truth – that the Art of making Sol and Luna is to be learnt. So, then, all these things should be passed by, because they have no effect with the five metals, so far as Sol and Luna are concerned. Someone may ask, What, then, is this short and easy way, which involves no difficulty, and yet whereby Sol and Luna can be made? Our answer is, this has been fully and openly explained in the Seven Canons. It would be lost labour should one seek further to instruct one who does not understand these. It would be impossible to convince such a person that these matters could be so easily understood, but in an occult rather than in an open sense.

THE ART IS THIS:

After you have made heaven, or the sphere of Saturn, with its life to run over the earth, place on it all the planets, or such, one or more, as you wish, so that the portion of Luna may be the smallest. Let all run, until heaven, or Saturn, has entirely disappeared. Then all those planets will remain dead with their old corruptible bodies, having meanwhile obtained another new, perfect, and incorruptible body.

That body is the spirit of heaven. From it these planets again receive a body and life, and live as before. Take this body from the life and the earth. Keep it. It is Sol and Luna. Here you have the Art altogether, clear and entire. If you do not yet understand it, or are not practised therein, it is well. It is better that it should be kept concealed, and not made public.

HOW TO CONJURE THE CRYSTAL SO THAT ALL THINGS MAY BE SEEN IN IT.

To conjure is nothing else than to observe anything rightly, to know and to understand what it is. The crystal is a figure of the air. Whatever appears in the air, movable or immovable, the same appears also in the speculum or crystal as a wave. For the air, the water, and the crystal, so far as vision is concerned, are one, like a mirror in which an inverted copy of an object is seen.

CONCERNING THE HEAT OF MERCURY.

Those who think that Mercury is of a moist and cold nature are plainly in error, because it is by its nature in the highest degree warm and moist, which is the cause of its being in a constant state of fluidity. If it were of a moist and cold nature it would have the appearance of frozen water, and be always hard and solid, so that it would be necessary to liquefy it by the heat of fire, as in the case of the other metals. But it does not require this, since it has liquidity and flux from its own heat naturally inborn in it, which keeps it in a state of perpetual fluidity and renders it "quick", so that it can neither die, nor be coagulated, nor congealed. And this is well worth noticing, that the spirits of the seven metals, or as many of them as have been commingled, as soon as they come into the fire, contend with one another, especially Mercury, so that each may put forth its powers and virtues in the endeavour to get the mastery in the way of liquefying and transmuting. One seizes on the virtue, life, and form of another, and assigns some other nature and form to this one. So then the spirits or vapours of the metals are stirred up by the heat to operate mutually one upon the other, and transmute from one virtue to another, until perfection and purity are attained.

But what must be done besides to Mercury in order that its moisture and heat may be taken away, and in their place such an extreme cold introduced as to congeal, consolidate, and altogether mortify the Mercury? Do what follows in the sentence subjoined: Take pure Mercury closely shut up in a silver pixis. Fill a jar with fragments of lead, in the midst of which place the pixis. Let it melt for twenty-four hours, that is, for a natural day. This takes away from Mercury his occult heat, adds an external heat, and contributes the internal coldness of Saturn and Luna (which are both planets of a cold nature), whence and whereby the Mercury is compelled to congeal, consolidate, and harden.

Note also that the coldness (which Mercury needs in its consolidation and mortification) is not perceptible by the external sense, as the cold of snow or of ice is, but rather, externally, there is a certain amount of apparent heat. Just in the same way is it with the heat of Mercury, which is the cause of its fluidity. It is not an external heat, perceptible in the same way as one of our qualities. Nay, externally a sort of coldness is perceptible. Whence the Sophists (a race which has more talk than true wisdom) falsely assert that Mercury is cold and of a moist nature, so that they go on and advise us to congeal it by means of heat; whereas heat only renders it more fluid, as they daily find out to their own loss rather than gain. True Alchemy which alone, by its unique Art, teaches how to fabricate Sol and Luna from the five imperfect metals, allows no other receipt than this, which well and truly says: Only from metals, in metals, by metals, and with metals, are perfect metals made, for in some things is Luna and in other metals is Sol.

WHAT MATERIALS AND INSTRUMENTS ARE REQUIRED IN ALCHEMY.

There is need of nothing else but a foundry, bellows, tongs, hammers, cauldrons, jars, and cupels made from beechen ashes. Afterwards, lay on Saturn, Jupiter, Mars, Sol, Venus, Mercury, and Luna. Let them operate finally up to Saturn.

THE METHOD OF SEEKING MINERALS.

The hope of finding these in the earth and in stones is most uncertain, and the labour very great. However, since this is the first mode of getting them, it is in no way to be despised, but greatly commended. Such a desire or appetite ought no more to be done away with than the lawful inclination of young people, and those in the prime of life, to matrimony. As the bees long for roses and other flowers for the purpose of making honey and wax, so, too, men – apart from avarice or their own aggrandisement – should seek to extract metal from the earth. He who does not seek it is not likely to find it. God dowers men not only with gold or silver, but also with poverty, squalor, and misery. He has given to some a singular knowledge of metals and minerals, whereby they have obtained an easier and shorter method of fabricating gold and silver, without digging and smelting them, than they were commonly accustomed to, by extracting them from their primitive bodies. And this is the case not only with subterranean substances, but by certain arts and knowledge they have extracted them from the five metals generally (that is to say, from metals excocted from minerals which are imperfect and called metals), viz., from

Mercury, Jupiter, Saturn, Mars and Venus, from all of which, and from each of them separately, Sol and Luna can be made, but from one more easily than from another. Note, that Sol and Luna can be made easily from Mercury, Saturn, and Jupiter, but from Mars and Venus with difficulty. It is possible to make them, however, but with the addition of Sol and Luna. Out of Magnesium and Saturn comes Luna, and out of Jupiter and Cinnabar pure Sol takes its rise. The skilful artist, however (how well I remember!), will be able by diligent consideration to prepare metals so that, led by a true method of reasoning, he can promote the perfection of metallic transformation more than do the courses of the twelve signs and the seven planets. In such matters it is quite superfluous to watch these courses, as also their aspects, good or bad days or hours, the prosperous or unlucky condition of this or that planet, for these matters can do no good, and much less can they do harm in the art of natural Alchemy. If otherwise, and you have a feasible process, operate when you please. If, however, there be anything wanting in you or your mode of working, or your understanding, the planets and the stars of heaven will fail you in your work.

If metals remain buried long enough in the earth, not only are they consumed by rust, but by long continuance they are even transmuted into natural stones, and there are a great many of these; but this is known to few. For there is found in the earth old stone money of the heathens, printed with their different figures. These coins were originally metallic, but through the transmutation brought about by Nature, they were turned into stone.

WHAT ALCHEMY IS.

Alchemy is nothing else but the set purpose, intention, and subtle endeavour to transmute the kinds of the metals from one to another.[10] According to this, each person, by his own mental grasp, can choose out for himself a better way and Art, and therein find truth, for the man who follows a thing up more intently does find the truth. It is highly necessary to have a correct estimation of stars and of stones, because the star is the informing spirit of all stones. For the Sol and Luna of all the celestial stars are nothing but one stone in itself; and the terrestrial stone has come forth from the celestial stone; through the same fire, coals, ashes, the same expulsions and repurgations as that celestial stone, it has been separated and brought, clear and pure in its brightness. The whole ball of the earth is only something thrown off, concrete, mixed, corrupted, ground, and again coagulated, and gradually liquefied into one mass, into a stony work, which has its seat and its rest in the midst of the firmamental sphere. Further it is to be remarked that those precious stones which shall forth-with be set down have the nearest place to the heavenly or sidereal ones in point of perfection, purity, beauty, brightness, virtue, power of withstanding fire, and incorruptibility, and they have been fixed with other stones in the earth.[11]

They have, therefore, the greatest affinity with heavenly stones and with the stars, because their natures are derived from these. They are found by men in a rude environment, and the common herd (whose property it is to take false views of things) believe that they were produced in the same place where they are found, and that they were afterwards polished, carried around, and sold, and accounted to be great riches, on account of their colours, beauty, and other virtues. A brief description of them follows:

The Emerald. This is a green transparent stone. It does good to the eyes and the memory. It defends chastity; and if this be violated by him who carries it, the stone itself does not remain perfect.[12]

The Adamant. A black crystal called Adamant or else Evax, on account of the joy which it is effectual in impressing on those who carry it. It is of an obscure and transparent blackness, the colour of iron. It is the hardest of all; but is dissolved in the blood of a goat. Its size at the largest does not exceed that of a hazel nut.[13]

The Magnet Is an iron stone, and so attracts iron to itself.[14]

The Pearl. The Pearl is not a stone, because it is produced in sea shells. It is of a white colour. Seeing that it grows in animated beings, in men or in fishes, it is not properly of a stony nature, but properly a depraved (otherwise a transmuted) nature supervening upon a perfect work.[15]

The Jacinth Is a yellow, transparent stone. There is a flower of the same name which, according to the fable of the poets, is said to have been a man.[16]

The Sapphire Is a stone of a celestial colour and a heavenly nature.[17]

The Ruby Shines with an intensely red nature.[18]

The Carbuncle. A solar stone, shining by its own nature like the sun.[19]

The Coral Is a white or red stone, not transparent. It grows in the sea, out of the nature of the water and the air, into the form of wood or a shrub; it hardens in the air, and is not capable of being destroyed in fire.[20]

The Chalcedony Is a stone made up of different colours, occupying a middle place between obscurity and transparency, mixed also with cloudiness, and liver coloured. It is the lowest of all the precious stones.[21]

The Topaz Is a stone shining by night. It is found among rocks.[22]

The Amethyst Is a stone of a purple and blood colour.[23]

The Chrysoprasus Is a stone which appears like fire by night, and like gold by day.

The Crystal Is a white stone, transparent, and very like ice. It is sublimated, extracted, and produced from other stones.[24]

As a pledge and firm foundation of this matter, note the following conclusion. If anyone intelligently and reasonably takes care to exercise himself in learning about the metals, what they are, and whence they are produced: he may know that our metals are nothing else than the best part and the spirit of common stones, that is, pitch, grease, fat, oil, and stone. But this is least pure, uncontaminated, and perfect, so long as it remains hidden or mixed with the stones. It should therefore be sought and found in the stones, be recognised in them, and extracted from them, that is, forcibly drawn out and liquefied. For then it is no longer a stone, but an elaborate and perfect metal, comparable to the stars of heaven, which are themselves, as it were, stones separated from those of earth.

Whoever, therefore, studies minerals and metals must be furnished with such reason and intelligence that he shall not regard only those common and known metals which are found in the depth of the mountains alone. For there is often found at the very surface of the earth such a metal as is not met with at all, or not equally good, in the depths. And so every stone which comes to our view, be it great or small, flint or simple rock, should be carefully investigated and weighed with a true balance, according to its nature and properties. Very often a common stone, thrown away and despised, is worth more than a cow. Regard must not always be had to the place of digging from which this stone came forth; for here the influence of the sky prevails. Everywhere there is presented to us earth, or dust, or sand, which often contain much gold or silver, and this you will mark.

HERE ENDS THE COELUM PHILOSOPHORUM.

NOTES

1. The three prime substances are proved only by fire, which manifests them pure, naked, clean, and simple. In the absence of all ordeal by fire, there is no proving of a substance possible. For fire tests everything, and when the impure matter is separated the three pure substances are displayed. – *De Origine Morborum ex Tribus Primis Substanstiis – Paramirum*, Lib. I., c. 1. Fire separates that which is constant or fixed from that which is fugitive or volatile. – *De Morbis Metallicis*, Lib. II., Tract I. Fire is the father or active principle of separation. – "Third Fragment on Tartar" from the *Fragmenta Medica*.

2. By the mediation of Vulcan, or fire, any metal can be generated from Mercury. At the same time, Mercury is imperfect as a metal; it is semi-generated and wanting in coagulation, which is the end of all metals. Up to the half way point of their generation all metals are Mercury. Gold, for example, is Mercury; but it loses the Mercurial nature by coagulation, and although the properties of Mercury are present in it, they are dead, for their vitality is destroyed by coagulation. – *De Morbis Metallicis*, Lib. III., Tract II., c. 2. The essences and arcanas which are latent in all the six metals are to be found in the substance of Mercury. – *Ibid.*, c. 3. There are two genera of Mercury, the fixed Mercury of earth and another kind which descends from the daily constellation. – *Ibid.*, Lib. I., Tract II., c. 4. As there is a red and white Sulphur of Marcasites, a yellow, red, and black Sulphur of Talc, a purple and black Sulphur of the Cachimiae, a Sulphur of Cinnabar, and, in like manner, of marble, amethyst, etc., so is there a special Mercury of Copper, Plumbago, Zinc, Arsenic, etc. – *Ibid*. Mercury is not Quicksilver, for Mercury is dead, while Quicksilver is living. –*De Hydropisi*.

3. Nothing of true value is located in the body of a substance, but in the virtue. And this is the principle of the Quintessence, which reduces, say, 20lbs. into a single ounce, and that ounce far exceeds the entire 20lbs. in potency. Hence the less there is of body, the more in proportion is the virtue. – *De Origine Morborum Invisibilium*, Lib. IV.

4 .Tin or Jupiter, is pure Mercury coagulated with a small quantity of Salt, but combined with a larger proportion of white Sulphur. It derives its colours, white, yellow, or red, from its Mercury. Its sublimation is also by Mercury, and its resolution by

Salt, and it is sublimed and resolved by these. – *De Elemento Aquae*, Tract III., c. 6.

5. In the generation of Iron there is a larger proportion of Salt and Mercury, while the red Sulphur from which copper proceeds is present in a smaller quantity. It contains also a cuprine salt, but not in equal proportion with Mercury. Its constituents are its own body, which preponderates; then comes Salt, afterwards Mercury, and, lastly, Sulphur. When there is more Salt than the composition of Sulphur requires, the metal can in no wise be made, for it depends upon an equal weight of each. For fluxibility proceeds from Mercury and coagulation from Salt. Accordingly, if there be too much Salt it becomes too hard. – *De Elemento Aquae*, Lib. I V., Tract III., c. 4.

6. Venus is the first metal generated by the Archeus of Nature from the three prime principles after the marcasites and cachimiae have been separated from these. It is formed of the gross redness which is purged off from the primal Sulphur of the light red expelled in like manner from the Mercury, and of the deep yellow separated in the purification of the prime Salt by this same Archeus. – *Ibid.*, c. 3.

7. Lead is the blackness of the three first principles, which, however, is by no means a superfluity, but a peculiar metallic nature in them existing. For all metals are latent in Mercury, and they are all only Mercury. The same is to be concluded concerning Salt and Sulphur. Thus, as copper is the abundant redness of the three principles, so Lead is their blackness; but, at the same time, there are four colours concealed therein – the blackness, purged off from the three principles; redness, which contains a precipitate out of Mercury; whiteness, from the calcination of Mercury; and a certain yellowness derived from Mercury. Thus the grossness and the colours are alike due to Mercury, and Lead is, in fact, a black Mercury. – *Ibid.*, c. 5.

8. When the three prime principles have been purged of their superfluities, and from the said superfluities the imperfect metals have been generated, there remains nothing gross or crude, either in colour or substance, but only a very subtle nature of a white and purple hue. This is the most pure quality of Mercury, Salt, and Sulphur, most clear and excellent in form, substance, essence, and colour. These two essences, namely, the white and the purple, are separated by the Archeus, and out of the first fixed and coagulated, is formed silver, while from the purple there is generated gold,

which is the most noble Sulphur, Salt, and Mercury, separated from all other colours, and consisting of purple alone. Its clayey or yellow appearance is accounted for by the subtlety and clearness of the metal, because all the dull colours are removed. In Silver the most prevalent colours are green and blue, which are respectively derived from the Mercury and the Salt, the Sulphur contributing nothing in the matter of colouring. On the other hand, in gold the purple colour is derived from Salt, the pellucid redness from Sulphur, and the yellow from Mercury. – *Ibid.*, c. 8.

9. Verbenas adole pingues, et mascula tura. – Virg., Ecl. viii. 65.

10. Alchemy is, so to speak, a kind of lower heaven, by which the sun is separated from the moon, day from night, medicine from poison, what is useful from what is refuse. – *De Colica*. Therefore learn Alchemy, which is otherwise called Spagyria. This teaches you to discern between the true and the false. Such a Light of Nature is it that it is a mode of proof in all things, and walks in light. From this light of Nature we ought to know and speak, not from mere phantasy, whence nothing is begotten save the four humours and their compounds, augmentation, stagnation, and decrease, with other trifles of this kind. These proceed, not from the clear intellect, that full treasure-house of a good man, but rather are based on a fictitious and insecure foundation. – *Paramirum*, Lib. I., c. 3.

11. When the occult dispenser of Nature in the prime principles that is to say, the potency called Ares, has produced the gross and rough genera of stones, and no further grossness remains, a diaphanous and subtle substance remains, out of which the Archeus of Nature generates the precious stones or gems. – *De Elemento Aquae*, Lib. IV., Tract IV., c. 10.

12. The body f the Emerald is derived from a kind of petrine Mercury. It receives from the same its colour, coagulated with spirit of Salt. – *Ibid.*, c. 12.

13. The most concentrated hardness of all stones combines for the generation of the adamant. The white adamant has its body from Mercury, and its coagulation from the spirit of Salt. – *Ibid*., c. 12.

14. Fortified by experience which is the mistress of all things, and by mature theory, based on experience, I affirm that the Magnet is a stone which not only undeniably attracts steel and iron, but has also the same power over the matter of all diseases in the whole body of man. – *De Corallis*. See *Herbarius Theophrasti*.

15. The Pearl is a seed of moisture. It generates milk abundantly in women if they are deficient therein. – *De Aridura*.

16. The Jacinth, or Hyacinth, is a gem of the same genus as the Carbuncle, but is inferior thereto in its nature. – *De Elemento Aquae*, Lib. IV., Tract IV., c. 11.

17. In the matter of body and colour the Sapphire is generated from Mercury (the prime principle). It is formed over white Sulphur and white Salt from a pallid petrine Mercury. Hence white Sapphires frequently occur because a white Mercury concurs in the formation. In like manner a lute-coloured Mercury sometimes produces a clay-like hue. – *Ibid.*, c. 15.

18. The Ruby and similar gems possessing a ruddy hue are generated from the red of Sulphur, and their body is of petrine Mercury. For Mercury is the body of every precious stone. – *Ibid.*, c. 13.

19. The Carbuncle is formed of the most transparent matter which is conserved in the three principles. Mercury is the body and Sulphur the colouring thereof, with a modicum of the spirit of Salt, on account of the coagulation. All light abounds therein, because Sulphur contains in itself a clear quality of light, as the art of its transmutation demonstrates. – *Ibid.*, c. 11.

20. There are two species of red Corals – one a dull red, which varies between sub-purple and semi-black; the other a resplendent and brilliant red. As the colours differ, so also do the virtues. There is also a whitish species which is almost destitute of efficacy. In a word, as the Coral diminishes in redness, so it weakens in its qualities. *Herbarius Theophrasti; De Corallis.*

21. The gem Chalcedony is extracted from Salt. – *Chirurgia Magna; De Tumoribus*, etc., *Morbi Gallici*, Lib. III., c. 6.

22. The Topaz is an extract from the minera of Mars, and is a transplanted Iron. – *Ibid.*

23. The Amethyst is an extract of Salt, while Marble and Chalcedony are extracted from the same principle through the Amethyst. – *Ibid.*

24. The origin of Crystals is to be referred to water. They contain within them a spirit of coagulation whereby they are coagulated, as water by the freezing and glacial stars. – *Lib. Meteorum*, c. 7.

THE BOOK CONCERNING THE TINCTURE OF THE
PHILOSOPHERS

WRITTEN AGAINST THOSE SOPHISTS BORN SINCE THE
DELUGE, IN THE AGE OF OUR LORD JESUS CHRIST, THE SON
OF GOD;

PH. THEOPHRASTUS BOMBAST, of HOHENHEIM,

Philosopher of the Monarchia, Prince of Spagyrists, Chief
Astronomer, Surpassing Physician, and Trismegistus of
Mechanical Arcana.

PREFACE.

Since you, O Sophist, everywhere abuse me with such fatuous and mendacious words, on the ground that being sprung from rude Helvetia I can understand and know nothing: and also because being a duly qualified physician I still wander from one district to another; therefore I have proposed by means of this treatise to disclose to the ignorant and inexperienced: what good arts existed in the first age; what my art avails against you and yours against me; what should be thought of each, and how my posterity in this age of grace will imitate me. Look at Hermes, Archelaus, and others in the first age: see what Spagyrists and what Philosophers then existed. By this they testify that their enemies, who are your patrons, O Sophist, at the present time are but mere empty forms and idols. Although this would not be attested by those who are falsely considered your authentic fathers and saints, yet the ancient Emerald Table shews more art and experience in Philosophy, Alchemy, Magic, and the like, than could ever be taught by you and your crowd of followers. If you do not yet understand, from the aforesaid facts, what and how great treasures these are, tell me why no prince or king was ever able to subdue the Egyptians. Then tell me why the Emperor Diocletian ordered all the Spagyric books to be burnt (so far as he could lay his hands upon them). Unless the contents of those books had been known, they would have been obliged to bear still his intolerable yoke, - a yoke, O Sophist, which shall one day be put upon the neck of yourself and your colleagues.

From the middle of this age the Monarchy of all the Arts has been at length derived and conferred on me, Theophrastus

Paracelsus, Prince of Philosophy and of Medicine. For this purpose I have been chosen by God to extinguish and blot out all the phantasies of elaborate and false works, of delusive and presumptuous words, be they the words of Aristotle, Galen, Avicenna, Mesva, or the dogmas of any among their followers. My theory, proceeding as it does from the light of Nature, can never, through its consistency, pass away or be changed: but in the fifty-eighth year after its millennium and a half it will then begin to flourish. The practice at the same time following upon the theory will be proved by wonderful and incredible signs, so as to be open to mechanics and common people, and they will thoroughly understand how firm and immovable is that Paracelsic Art against the triflings of the Sophists: though meanwhile that sophistical science has to have its ineptitude propped up and fortified by papal and imperial privileges. In that I am esteemed by you a mendicant and vagabond sophist, the Danube and the Rhine will answer that accusation, though I hold my tongue. Those calumnies of yours falsely devised against me have often displeased many courts and princes, many imperial cities, the knightly order, and the nobility. I have a treasure hidden in a certain city called Weinden, belonging to Forum Julii, at an inn, - a treasure which neither you, Leo of Rome, nor you, Charles the German, could purchase with all your substance. Although the signed star has been applied to the arcanum of your names, it is known to none but the sons of the divine Spagyric Art. So then, you wormy and lousy Sophist, since you deem the monarch of arcana a mere ignorant, fatuous, and prodigal quack, now, in this mid age, I determine in my present treatise to disclose the honourable course of procedure in these matters, the virtues and preparation of the celebrated Tincture of the Philosophers for the use and honour of all who love the truth, and in order that all who despise the true arts may be reduced to poverty. By this arcanum the last age shall be illuminated clearly and compensated for all its losses by the gift of grace and the reward of the spirit of truth, so that since the beginning of the world no similar germination of the intelligence and of wisdom shall ever have been heard of. In the meantime, vice will not be able to suppress the good, nor will the resources of those vicious persons, many though they be, cause any loss to the upright.

CHAPTER I.

I, PHILIPPUS Theophrastus Paracelsus Bombast, say that, by Divine grace, many ways have been sought to the Tincture of the Philosophers, which finally all came to the same scope and end. Hermes Trismegistus, the Egyptian, approached this task in his own method. Orus, the Greek, observed the same process. Hali, the Arabian, remained firm in his order. But Albertus Magnus, the German, followed also a lengthy process. Each one of these advanced in proportion to his own method; nevertheless, they all arrive at one and the same end, at a long life, so much desired by the philosophers, and also at an honourable sustenance and means of preserving that life in this Valley of Misery. Now at this time, I, Theophrastus Paracelsus Bombast, Monarch of the Arcana, am endowed by God with special gifts for this end, that every searcher after this supreme philosophic work may be forced to imitate and to follow me, be he Italian, Pole, Gaul, German, or whatsoever or whosoever he be. Come hither after me, all you philosophers, astronomers, and spagyrists, of however lofty a name ye may be, I will show and open to you, Alchemists and Doctors, who are exalted by me with the most consummate labours, this corporeal regeneration. I will teach you the tincture, the arcanum, the quintessence, wherein lie hid the foundations of all mysteries and of all works. For every person may and ought to believe in another only in those matters, which he has tried by fire. If any one shall have brought forward anything contrary to this method of experimentation in the Spagyric Art or in Medicine, there is no reason for your belief in him, since, experimentally, through the agency of fire, the true is separated from the false.

The light of Nature indeed is created in this way, that by means thereof the proof or trial of everything may appear, but only to those who walk in this light. With this light we will teach, by the very best methods of demonstration, that all those who before me have approached this so difficult province with their own fancies and acute speculations have, to their own loss, incurred the danger of their foolishness. On which account, from my standpoint, many rustics have been ennobled; but, on the other hand, through the speculative and opinionative art of these many nobles have been changed into clowns, and since they carried golden mountains in their head before they had put their hand to the fire. First of all, then, there must be learnt - digestions, distillations, sublimations, reverberations, extractions, solutions, coagulations, fermentations, fixations, and every instrument which is requisite for this work must be mastered by experience, such as glass vessels, cucurbites, circulators, vessels of Hermes, earthen vessels, baths, blast-furnaces, reverberatories, and instruments of like kind, also marble, coals, and tongs. Thus at length you will be able to profit in Alchemy and in Medicine.

But so long as, relying on fancy and opinion, you cleave to your fictitious books, you are fitted and predestinated for no one of these things.

CHAPTER II.

CONCERNING THE DEFINITION OF THE SUBJECT AND MATTER OF THE TINCTURE OF THE PHILOSOPHERS.

Before I come, then, to the process of the Tincture, it is needful that I open to you the subject thereof: for, up to the present time, this has always been kept in a specially occult way by the lovers of truth. So, then, the matter of the Tincture (when you understand me in a Spagyrical sense) is a certain thing which, by the art of Vulcan2, passes out of three essences into one essence, or it may remain. But, that I may give it its proper name, according to the use of the ancients, though it is called by many the Red Lion, still it is known by few. This, by the aid of Nature and the skill of the Artist himself, can be transmuted into a White Eagle, so that out of one two are produced; and beyond this the brightness of gold does not shine so much for the Spagyrist as do these two when kept in one. Now, if you do not understand the use of the Cabalists and the old astronomers, you are not born by God for the Spagyric art, or chosen by Nature for the work of Vulcan, or created to open your mouth concerning Alchemical Arts. The matter of the Tincture, then, is a very great pearl and a most precious treasure, and the noblest thing next to the manifestation of the Most High and the consideration of men which can exist upon earth. This is the Lili of Alchemy and of Medicine, which the philosophers have so diligently sought after, but, through the failure of entire knowledge and complete preparation, they have not progressed to the perfect end thereof. By means of their investigations and experiments, only the initial stage of the Tincture has been given to us; but the true foundation, which my colleagues must imitate, has been left for me, so that no one should mingle their shadows with our good intentions. I, by right after my long experiences, correct the Spagyrists, and separate the false or the erroneous from the true, since, by long investigations, I have found reasons why I should be able justly to blame and to change diverse things. If, indeed, I had found out experiments of the ancients better than my own, I should scarcely have taken up such great labours as, for the sake, the utility, and the advantage of all good Alchemists, I have undergone willingly. Since, then, the subject of the Tincture has been sufficiently declared, so that it scarcely could or ought to be exceeded in fidelity between two brothers, I approach its preparation, and after I have laid down the experiences of the first age, I wish to add my own inventions; to which at last the Age of Grace will by-and-by give its adhesion, whichever of the patriarchs, O Sophist, you, in the meantime, shall have made leaders.

CHAPTER III.

CONCERNING THE PROCESS OF THE ANCIENTS FOR THE TINCTURE OF THE PHILOSOPHERS, AND A MORE COMPENDIOUS METHOD BY PARACELSUS.

The old Spagyrists putrefied Lili for a philosophical month, and afterwards distilled therefrom the moist spirits, until at length the dry spirits were elevated. They again imbued the caput mortuum with moist spirits, and drew them off from it frequently by distillation until the dry spirits were all elevated. Then afterwards they united the moisture that had been drawn off and the dry spirits by means of a pelican, three or four times, until the whole Lili remained dry at the bottom. Although early experience gave this process before fixation, none the less our ancestors often attained a perfect realisation of their wish by this method. They would, however, have had a shorter way of arriving at the treasure of the Red Lion if they had learnt the agreement of Astronomy with Alchemy, as I have demonstrated it in the Apocalypse of Hermes3. But since every day (as Christ says for the consolation of the faithful) has its own peculiar care, the labour for the Spagyrists before my times has been great and heavy; but this, by the help of the Holy Spirit flowing into us, will, in this last age, be lightened and made clear by my theory and practice, for all those who constantly persevere in their work with patience. For I have tested the properties of Nature, its essences and conditions, and I know its conjunction and resolution, which are the highest and greatest gift for a philosopher, and never understood by the sophists up to this time. When, therefore, the earliest age gave the first experience of the Tincture, the Spagyrists made two things out of one simple. But when afterwards, in the Middle Age, this invention had died out, their successors by diligent scrutiny afterwards came upon the two names of this simple, and they named it with one word, namely, Lili, as being the subject of the Tincture. At length the imitators of Nature putrefied this matter at its proper period just like the seed in the earth, since before this corruption nothing could be born from it, nor any arcanum break forth from it. Afterwards they drew off the moist spirits from the matter, until at length, by the violence of the fire, the dry were also equally sublimated, so that, in this way, just as the rustic does at the proper time of year, they might come to maturity as one after another is wont to ascend and to fall away. Lastly, as after the spring comes summer, they incorporated those fruits and dry spirits, and brought the Magistery of the Tincture to such a point that it came to the harvest, and laid itself out for ripening.

CHAPTER IV.

CONCERNING THE PROCESS FOR THE TINCTURE OF THE PHILOSOPHERS, AS IT IS SHORTENED BY PARACELSUS.

The ancient Spagyrists would not have required such lengthened labour and such wearisome repetition if they had learnt and practised their work in my school. They would have obtained their wish just as well, with far less expense and labour. But at this time, when Theophrastus Paracelsus has arrived as the Monarch of Arcana, the opportunity is at hand for finding out those things which were occult to all Spagyrists before me. Wherefore I say, Take only the rose-coloured blood from the Lion and the gluten from the Eagle. When you have mixed these, coagulate them according to the old process, and you will have the Tincture of the Philosophers, which an infinite number have sought after and very few have found. Whether you will or not, sophist, this Magistery is in Nature itself, a wonderful thing of God above Nature, and a most precious treasure in this Valley of Sorrows. If you look at it from without it seems a paltry thing to transmute another into something far more noble than it was before. But you must, nevertheless, allow this, and confess that it is a miracle produced by the Spagyrist, who by the art of his preparation corrupts a visible body which is externally vile, from which he excites another most noble and most precious essence. If you, in like manner, have learnt anything from the light of Aristotle, or from us, or from the rules of Serapio, come forth, and bring that knowledge experimentally to light. Preserve now the right of the Schools, as becomes a lover of honour and a doctor.

But if you know nothing and can do nothing, why do you despise me as though I were an irrational Helvetian cow, and inveigh against me as a wandering vagabond? Art is a second Nature and a universe of its own, as experience witnesses, and demonstrates against you and your idols. Sometimes, therefore, the Alchemist compounds certain simples, which he afterwards corrupts according to his need, and prepares thence another thing. For thus very often out of many things one is made, which effects more than Nature of herself can do, as in Gastaynum it is perfectly well known that Venus is produced from Saturn; in Carinthia, Luna out of Venus; and in Hungary, Sol out of Luna; to pass over in silence for the time being the transmutations of other natural objects, which were well known to the Magi, and more wonderfully than Ovid narrates in his Metamorphoses do they come to the light. That you may rightly understand me, seek your Lion in the East, and your Eagle in the South, for this our work which has been undertaken. You will not find better instruments than Hungary and Istria produce. But if you desire to lead from unity by duality in trinity with equal permutation of each, then you should direct your journey to the South; so in Cyprus shall you gain all your desire, concerning which we must not dilate more profusely than we have done at present. There are still many more of these arcana which exhibit transmutations, though they are known to few. And although these may by the Lord God be made manifest to anyone, still, the rumour of this Art does not on that account at once break forth, but the Almighty gives therewith the understanding how to conceal these and other like arts even to the coming of Elias the Artist, at which time there shall be nothing so occult that it shall not be revealed. You also see with your eyes (though there is no need to speak of these things, which may be taken derisively by some) that in the fire of Sulphur is a great tincture for gems, which, indeed, exalts them to a loftier degree than Nature by herself could do. But this gradation of metals and gems shall be omitted by me in this place, since I have written sufficiently about it in my Secret of Secrets, in my book on the Vexations of Alchemists, and abundantly elsewhere. As I have begun the process of our ancestors with the Tincture of the Philosophers, I will now perfectly conclude it.

CHAPTER V.

CONCERNING THE CONCLUSION OF THE PROCESS OF THE ANCIENTS, MADE BY PARACELSUS.

Lastly, the ancient Spagyrists having placed Lili in a pelican and dried it, fixed it by means of a regulated increase of the fire, continued so long until from blackness, by permutation into all the colours, it became red as blood, and therewith assumed the condition of a salamander. Rightly, indeed, did they proceed with such labour, and in the same way it is right and becoming that everyone should proceed who seeks this pearl. It will be very difficult for me to make this clearer to you unless you shall have learnt in the School of the Alchemists to observe the degrees of the fire, and also to change your vessels. For then at length you will see that soon after your Lili shall have become heated in the Philosophic Egg, it becomes, with wonderful appearances, blacker than the crow; afterwards, in succession of time, whiter than the swan; and at last, passing through a yellow colour, it turns out more red than any blood. Seek, seek, says the first Spagyrist, and you shall find; knock, and it shall be opened unto you. It would be impious and indecorous to put food in the mouth of a perfidious bird. Let her rather fly to it, even as I, with others before me, have been compelled to do. But follow true Art; for this will lead you to its perfect knowledge. It is not possible that anything should here be set down more fully or more clearly than I have before spoken. Let your Pharisaical schools teach you what they will from their unstable and slippery foundation, which reaches not its end or its aim. When at length you shall have been taught as accurately as possible the Alchemistic Art, nothing in the nature of things shall then at length be so difficult which cannot be made manifest to you by the aid of this Art. Nature, indeed, herself does not bring forth anything into the light which is advanced to its highest perfection, as can be seen in this place from the unity, or the union, of our duality. But a man ought by Spagyric preparations to lead it thither where it was ordained by Nature. Let this have been sufficiently said by me, concerning the process of the ancients and my correction of the Tincture of the Philosophers, so far as relates to its preparation.

Moreover, since now we have that treasure of the Egyptians in our hands, it remains that we turn it to our use: and this is offered to us by the Spagyric Magistery in two ways. According to the former mode it can be applied for the renewing of the body; according to the latter it is to be used for the transmutation of metals. Since, then, I, Theophrastus Paracelsus, have tried each of them in different ways, I am willing to put them forward and to describe them according to the signs indeed of the work, and as in experience and proof they appeared to me better and more perfectly.

CHAPTER VI.

CONCERNING THE TRANSMUTATION OF METALS BY THE PERFECTION OF MEDICINE.

If the Tincture of the Philosophers is to be used for transmutation, a pound of it must be projected on a thousand pounds of melted Sol. Then, at length, will a Medicine have been prepared for transmuting the leprous moisture of the metals. This work is a wonderful one in the light of Nature, namely, that by the Magistery, or the operation of the Spagyrist, a metal, which formerly existed, should perish, and another be produced. This fact has rendered that same Aristotle, with his ill-founded philosophy, fatuous. For truly, when the rustics in Hungary cast iron at the proper season into a certain fountain, commonly called Zifferbrunnen, it is consumed into rust, and when this is liquefied with a blast-fire, it soon exists as pure Venus, and never more returns to iron. Similarly, in the mountain commonly called Kuttenberg, they obtain a lixivium out of marcasites, in which iron is forthwith turned into Venus of a high grade, and more malleable than the other produced by Nature. These things, and more like them, are known to simple men rather than to sophists, namely, those which turn one appearance of a metal into another. And these things, moreover, through the remarkable contempt of the ignorant, and partly, too, on account of the just envy of the artificers, remain almost hidden. But I myself, in Istria, have often brought Venus to more than twenty-four (al. 38) degrees, so that the colour of Sol could not mount higher, consisting of Antimony or or Quartal, which Venus I used in all respects as other kinds.

But though the old artists were very desirous of this arcanum, and sought it with the greatest diligence, nevertheless, very few could bring it by means of a perfect preparation to its end. For the transmutation of an inferior metal into a superior one brings with it many difficulties and obstacles, as the change of Jove into Luna, or Venus into Sol. Perhaps on account of their sins God willed that the Magnalia of Nature should be hidden from many men. For sometimes, when this Tincture has been prepared by artists, and they were not able to reduce their projection to work its effects, it happened that, by their carelessness and bad guardianship, this was eaten up by fowls, whose feathers thereupon fell off, and, as I myself have seen, grew again. In this way transmutation, through its abuse from the carelessness of the artists, came into Medicine and Alchemy. For when they were unable to use the Tincture according to their desire, they converted the same to the renovation of men, as shall be heard more at large in the following chapter.

CHAPTER VII.

CONCERNING THE RENOVATION OF MEN.

Some of the first and primitive philosophers of Egypt have lived by means of this Tincture for a hundred and fifty years. The life of many, too, has been extended and prolonged to several centuries, as is most clearly shewn in different histories, though it seems scarcely credible to any one. For its power is so remarkable that it extends the life of the body beyond what is possible to its congenital nature, and keeps it so firmly in that condition that it lives on in safety from all infirmities. And although, indeed, the body at length comes to old age, nevertheless, it still appears as though it were established in its primal youth.

So, then, the Tincture of the Philosophers is a Universal Medicine, and consumes all diseases, by whatsoever name they are called, just like an invisible fire. The dose is very small, but its effect is most powerful. By means thereof I have cured the leprosy, venereal disease, dropsy, the falling sickness, colic, scab, and similar afflictions; also lupus, cancer, noli-me-tangere, fistulas, and the whole race of internal diseases, more surely than one could believe. Of this fact Germany, France, Italy, Poland, Bohemia, etc., will afford the most ample evidence.

Now, Sophist, look at Theophrastus Paracelsus. How can your Apollo, Machaon, and Hippocrates stand against me? This is the Catholicum of the Philosophers, by which all these philosophers have attained long life for resisting diseases, and they have attained this end entirely and most effectually, and so, according to their judgment, they named it The Tincture of the Philosophers. For what can there be in the whole range of medicine greater than such purgation of the body, by means whereof all superfluity is radically removed from it and transmuted? For when the seed is once made sound all else is perfected. What avails the ill-founded purgation of the sophists since it removes nothing as it ought? This, therefore, is the most excellent foundation of a true physician, the regeneration of the nature, and the restoration of youth. After this, the new essence itself drives out all that is opposed to it. To effect this regeneration, the powers and virtues of the Tincture of the Philosophers were miraculously discovered, and up to this time have been used in secret and kept concealed by true Spagyrists.

HERE ENDS THE BOOK CONCERNING THE TINCTURE OF THE PHILOSOPHERS.

NOTES

1 The Arcanum of a substance is not the virtue (*virtus*) but the essence (*vir*) and the potency (*potentia*), and is stronger than the virtue; nevertheless, an old error of the doctors conferred the name of virtues upon the potential essences. - *Paramirum*, Lib. IV. Many things are elsewhere set forth concerning the Quintessence, but what is described is really a separation or extraction of the pure from the impure, not a true quintessence, and it is more correctly termed an Arcanum. -*Explicatio Totius Astronomiae.*

2 The office of Vulcan is the separation of the good from the bad. So the Art of Vulcan, which is Alchemy, is like unto death, by which the eternal and the temporal are divided one from another. So also this art might be called the death of things. - *De Morbis Metallicis*, Lib. I., Tract III., c. 1. Vulcan is an astral and not a corporal fabricator. - *De Caduco Matricis*, Par. VI. The artist working in metals and other minerals transforms them into other colours, and in so doing his operation is like that of the heaven itself. For as the artist excocts by means of Vulcan, or the igneous element, so heaven performs the work of coction through the Sun. The Sun, therefore, is the Vulcan of heaven accomplishing coction in the earth. - *De Icteritiis*. Vulcan is the fabricator and architect of all things, nor is his habitation in heaven only, that is, in the firmament, but equally in all the other elements. - *Lib. Meteorum*, c. 4. Where the three prime principles are wanting, there also the igneous essence is absent. The Igneous Vulcan is nothing else but Sulphur, Sal Nitrum, and Mercury. - *Ibid.*, c.5.

3 The Book of the Revelation of Hermes, interpreted by Theophrastus Paracelsus, concerning the Supreme Secret of the World, seems to have been first brought to light by Benedictus Figulus, and appeared as a *piece de résistance* in his "Golden and Blessed Casket of Nature's Marvels", of which an English translation has been very recently published. ("A Golden and Blessed Casket of Nature's Marvels". By Benedictus Figulus. Now first done into English from the German original published at Frankfort in the year 1608. London: James Elliott and Co. 8vo., 1893). Among the many writings which have been fabulously attributed to Hermes, there does not seem to be any record of an apocalypse, and it is impossible to say what forged document may have been the subject of interpretation by Paracelsus. As the collection of Figulus is now so readily accessible, it is somewhat

superfluous to reproduce the treatise here, but since this translation claims to include everything written by the physician of Hohenheim on the subject of Alchemy and the Universal Medicine, it is appended at this point. It should be premised that Benedictus Figulus complains bitterly of the mutilation and perversion to which the works of Paracelsus were subjected, and the Revelation of Hermes seems in many parts to betray another hand, especially in its quotation of authorities who are not countenanced by its reputed author. Hermes, Plato, Aristotle, and other philosophers, flourishing at different times, who have introduced the Arts, and more especially have explored the secrets of inferior Creation, all these have eagerly sought a means whereby man's body might be preserved from decay and become endued with immortality. To them it was answered that there is nothing which might deliver the mortal body from death; but that there is One Thing which may postpone decay, renew youth; and prolong short human life (as with the patriarchs). For death was laid as a punishment upon our first parents, Adam and Eve, and will never depart from all their descendants. Therefore, the above philosophers, and many others, have sought this One Thing with great labour, and have found that that which preserves the human body from corruption, and prolongs life, conducts itself, with respect to other elements, as it were like the Heavens; from which they understood that the Heavens are a substance above the Four Elements. And just as the Heavens, with respect to the other elements, are held to be the fifth substance (for they are indestructible, stable, and suffer no foreign admixture), so also this One Thing (compared to the forces of our body) is an indestructible essence, drying up all the superfluities of our bodies, and has been philosophically called by the above-mentioned name. It is neither hot and dry like fire, nor cold and moist like water, nor warm and moist like air, nor dry and cold like earth. But it is a skilful, perfect equation of all the Elements, a right commingling of natural forces, a most particular union of spiritual virtues, an indissoluble uniting of body and soul. It is the purest and noblest substance of an indestructible body, which cannot be destroyed nor harmed by the Elements, and is produced by Art. With this, Aristotle prepared an apple, prolonging life by its scent, when he, fifteen days before his death, could neither eat nor drink on account of old age. This spiritual Essence, or One Thing, was revealed from above to Adam, and was greatly desired by the Holy

Fathers; this also Hermes and Aristotle call the Truth without Lies, the most sure of all things certain, the Secret of all Secrets. It is the Last and the Highest Thing to be sought under the Heavens, a wondrous closing and finish of philosophical work, by which are discovered the dews of Heaven and the fastnesses of Earth. What the mouth of man cannot utter is all found in this spirit. As Morienus says: "He who has this has all things, and wants no other aid. For in it are all temporal happiness, bodily health, and earthly fortune. It is the spirit of the fifth substance, a Fount of all Joys (beneath the rays of the moon), the Supporter of Heaven and Earth, the Mover of Sea and Wind, the Outpourer of Rain, upholding the strength of all things, an excellent spirit above Heavenly and other spirits, giving Health, Joy, Peace, Love; driving away Hatred and Sorrow, bringing in Joy, expelling all Evil, quickly healing all Diseases, destroying Poverty and misery, leading to all good things, preventing all evil words and thoughts, giving man his heart's desire, bringing to the pious earthly honour and long life, but to the wicked who misuse it, Eternal Punishment". This is the Spirit of Truth, which the world cannot comprehend without the interposition of the Holy Ghost, or without the instruction of those who know it. The same is of a mysterious nature, wondrous strength, boundless power. The Saints, from the beginning of the world, have desired to behold its face. By Avicenna this Spirit is named the Soul of the World. For, as the Soul moves all the limbs of the body, so also does this Spirit move all bodies. And as the Soul is in all the limbs of the Body, so also is this Spirit in all elementary created things. It is sought by many and found by few. It is beheld from afar and found near; for it exists in every thing, in every place, and at all times. It has the powers of all creatures; its action is found in all elements, and the qualities of all things are therein, even in the highest perfection. By virtue of this essence did Adam and the Patriarchs preserve their health and live to an extreme age, some of them also flourishing in great riches. When the philosophers had discovered it, with great diligence and labour, they straightway concealed it under a strange tongue, and in parables, lest the same should become known to the unworthy, and the pearls be cast before swine. For if everyone knew it, all work and industry would cease; man would desire nothing but this one thing, people would live wickedly, and the world be ruined, seeing that they would provoke God by reason of their avarice and superfluity. For eye hath not seen, nor ear heard, nor hath the heart of man understood what Heaven hath naturally incorporated with this Spirit. Therefore have I briefly enumerated some of the qualities of this Spirit, to the Honour of God, that the pious may reverently praise Him in His gifts (which gift of God shall afterwards come to them), and I will herewith shew what powers and virtues it possesses in each thing, also its outward appearance, that it may be more readily recognised. In its first state, it appears as an impure earthly body, full of imperfections. It then has an earthly nature, healing all sickness and wounds in the bowels of man, producing good and consuming proud flesh, expelling all stench, and healing generally, inwardly and outwardly. In its second nature, it appears as a watery body, somewhat more beautiful than before, because (although still having its corruptions) its Virtue is greater. It is much nearer the truth, and more effective in works. In this form it cures cold and hot fevers and is a specific against poisons, which it drives from heart and lungs, healing the same when injured or wounded, purifying the blood, and, taken three times a day, is of great comfort in all diseases. But in its third nature it appears as an aerial body, of an oily nature, almost freed from all imperfections, in which form it does many wondrous works, producing beauty and strength of body, and (a small quantity being taken in the food) preventing melancholy and heating of the gall, increasing the quantity of the blood and seed, so that frequent bleeding becomes necessary. It expands the blood vessels, cures withered limbs, restores strength to the sight, in growing persons removes what is superfluous and makes good defects in the limbs. In its fourth nature it appears in a fiery form (not quite freed from all imperfections, still somewhat watery and not dried enough), wherein it has many virtues, making the old young and reviving those at the point of death. For if to such an one there be given, in wine, a barleycorn's weight of this fire, so that it reach the stomach, it goes to his heart, renewing him at once, driving away all previous moisture and poison, and restoring the natural heat of the liver. Given in small doses to old people, it removes the diseases of age, giving the old young hearts and bodies. Hence it is called the Elixir of Life. In its fifth and last nature, it appears in a glorified and illuminated form, without defects, shining like gold and silver, wherein it possesses all previous powers and virtues in a higher and more wondrous degree. Here its natural works are taken for miracles. When applied to the roots of dead trees they revive, bringing forth leaves and fruit. A lamp, the oil of which is mingled with this spirit, continues to burn for ever without diminution. It converts crystals into the most precious stones of all colours, equal to those from the mines, and does mayn other incredible wonders which may not be revealed to the unworthy. For it heals all dead and living bodies without other medicine. Here Christ is my witness that I lie not, for all heavenly influences are united and combined therein. This essence also reveals all treasures in earth and sea, converts all metallic bodies into gold, and there is nothing like unto it under Heaven. This spirit is the secret hidden from the beginning, yet granted by God to a few holy men for the revealing of these iches to His Glory - dwelling in fiery form in the air, and leading earth with itself to heaven, while from its body there flow whole rivers of living water. This spirit flies through the midst of the Heavens like a morning mist, leads its burning fire into the water, and has its shining realm in the heavens. And although these writings may be regarded as false by the reader, yet to the initiated they are true and possible, when the hidden sense is properly understood. For God is wonderful in His works, and His wisdom is without end. This spirit in its fiery form is called a Sandaraca, in the aerial a Kybrick, in the watery an Azoth, in the earthly Alcohoph and Aliocosoph. Hence they are deceived by these names who, seeking without instruction, think to find this Spirit of Life in things foreign to our Art. For although this spirit which we seek, on account of its qualities, is called by these names, yet the same is not in these bodies and cannot be in them. For a refined spirit cannot appear except in a body suitable to its nature. And, by however many names it be called, let no one imagine there be different spirits, for, say what one will, there is but one spirit working everywhere and in all things. That is the spirit which, when rising, illumines the Heavens, when setting incorporates the purity of Earth, and when brooding has embraced the Waters. This spirit is named Raphael, the Angel of God, the subtlest and purest, whom the others all obey as their King. This spiritual substance is neither heavenly nor hellish, but an airy, pure, and hearty body, midway between the highest and lowest, without reason, but fruitful in works, and the most select and beautiful of all other heavenly things. This work of God is far too deep for understanding, for it is the last, greatest, and highest secret of Nature. It is the Spirit of God, which in the Beginning filled the earth and brooded over the waters, which the world cannot grasp without the gracious interposition of the Holy Spirit and instruction from those who know it, which also the whole world desires for its virtue, and which cannot be prized enough. For it reaches to the planets, raises the clouds, drives away mists, gives its light to all things, turns everything into Sun and Moon, bestows all health and abundance of treasure, cleanses the leper, brightens the eyes, banishes sorrow, heals the sick, reveals all hidden treasures, and, generally, cures all diseases. Through this spirit have the philosophers invented the Seven Liberal Arts, and thereby gained their riches. Through the same Moses made the golden vessels in the Ark, and King Solomon did many beautiful works to the honour of God. Therewith Moses built the Tabernacle, Noah the Ark, Solomon the Temple. By this, Ezra restored the Law, and Miriam, Moses' sister, was hospitable; Abraham, Isaac, and Jacob, and other righteous men, have had lifelong abundance and riches; and all the saints possessing it have therewith praised God. Therefore is its acquisition very hard, more than that of gold and silver. For it is the best of all things, because, of all things mortal that man can desire in this world, nothing can compare with it, and in it alone is truth. Hence it is called the Stone and Spirit of Truth; in its works is no vanity, its praise cannot be sufficiently expressed. I am unable to speak enough of its virtues, because its good qualities and powers are beyond human thoughts, unutterable by the tongue of man, and in it are found the properties of all things. Yea, there is nothing deeper in Nature. O unfathomable abyss of God's Wisdom, which thus hath united and comprised in the virtue and power of this One Spirit the qualities of all existing bodies! O unspeakable honour and boundless joy granted to mortal man! For the destructible things of Nature are restored by virtue of the said Spirit. O mystery of mysteries, most secret of all secret things, and healing and medicine of all things! Thou last discovery in earthly natures, last best gift to Patriarchs and Sages, greatly desired by the whole world! Oh, what a wondrous and laudable spirit is purity, in which stand all joy, riches, fruitfulness of life, and art of all arts, a power which to its initiates grants all material joys! O desirable knowledge, lovely above all things beneath the circle of the Moon, by which Nature is strengthened, and heart and limbs are renewed, blooming youth is preserved, old age driven away, weakness destroyed, beauty in its perfection preserved, and abundance ensured in all things pleasing to men! O thou spiritual substance, lovely above all things! O thou wondrous power, strengthening all the world! O thou invincible virtue, highest of all that is, although despised by the ignorant, yet held by the wise in great praise, honour, and glory, that - proceeding from humours - wakest the dead, expellest diseases, restorest the voice of the dying! O thou treasure of treasures, mystery of mysteries, called by Avicenna "an unspeakable substance", the purest and most perfect soul of the world, than which there is nothing more costly under Heaven, unfathomable in nature and power, wonderful in virtue and works, having no equal among creatures, possessing the virtues of all bodies under Heaven! For from it flow the water of life, the oil and honey of eternal healing, and thus hath it nourished them with honey and water from the rock. Therefore, saith Morienus: "He who hath it, the same also hath all things". Blessed art Thou, Lord God of our Fathers, in that Thou hast given the prophets this knowledge and understanding, that they have hidden these things (lest they should be discovered by the blind, and those drowned in worldly godlessness) by which the wise and the pious have praised Thee! For the discoverers of the mystery of this thing to the unworthy are breakers of the seal of Heavenly Revelation, thereby offending God's Majesty, and bringing upon themselves many misfortunes and the punishments of God. Therefore, I beg all Christians, possessing this knowledge, to communicate the same to nobody, except it be to one living in Godliness, of well-proved virtue, and praising God, Who has given such a treasure to man. For many seek, but few find it. Hence the impure and those living in vice are unworthy of it. Therefore is this Art to be shewn to all God-fearing persons, because it cannot be bought with a price. I testify before God that I lie not, although it appear impossible to fools, that no one has hitherto explored Nature so deeply. The Almighty be praised for having created this Art and for revealing it to God-fearing men. Amen. And thus is fulfilled this precious and excellent work, called the revealing of the occult spirit, in which lie hidden the secrets and mysteries of the world. But this spirit is one genius, and divine, wonderful, and lordly power. For it embraces the whole world, and overcomes the Elements and the fifth Substance. To our Trismegistus Spagyrus, Jesus Christ, be praise and glory immortal. Amen.

The Treasure of Treasures for Alchemists.

The Treasure of Treasures for Alchemists.

Philippus Theophrastus Bombast, Paracelsus the Great

Nature begets a mineral in the bowels of the earth. There are two kinds of it, which are found in many districts of Europe. The best which has been offered to me, which also has been found genuine in experimentation, is externally in the figure of the greater world, and is in the eastern part of the sphere of the Sun. The other, in the Southern Star, is now in its first efflorescence. The bowels of the earth thrust this forth through its surface. It is found red in its first coagulation, and in it lie hid all the flowers and colours of the minerals. Much has been written about it by the philosophers, for it is of a cold and moist nature, and agrees with the element of water.

So far as relates to the knowledge of it and experiment with it, all the philosophers before me, though they have aimed at it with their missiles, have gone very wide of the mark. They believed that Mercury and Sulphur were the mother of all metals, never even dreaming of making mention meanwhile of a third; and yet when the water is separated from it by Spagyric Art the truth is plainly revealed, though it was unknown to Galen or to Avicenna. But if, for the sake of our excellent physicians, we had to describe only the name, the composition; the dissolution, and coagulation, as in the beginning of the world Nature proceeds with all growing things, a whole year would scarcely suffice me, and, in order to explain these things, not even the skins of numerous cows would be adequate.

Now, I assert that in this mineral are found three principles, which are Mercury, Sulphur, and the Mineral Water which has served to naturally coagulate it. Spagyric science is able to extract this last from its proper juice when it is not altogether matured, in the middle of the autumn, just like a pear from a tree. The tree potentially contains the pear. If the Celestial Stars and Nature agree, the tree first of all puts forth shoots in the month of March; then it thrusts out buds, and when these open the flower appears, and so on in due order until in autumn the pear grows ripe. So is it with the minerals. These are born, in like manner, in the bowels of the earth. Let the Alchemists who are seeking the Treasure of Treasures carefully note this. I will shew them the way, its beginning, its middle, and its end. In the following treatise I will describe the proper Water, the proper Sulphur, and the proper Balm thereof. By means of these three the resolution and composition are coagulated into one.

CONCERNING THE SULPHUR OF CINNABAR.

Take mineral Cinnabar and prepare it in the following manner. Cook it with rain water in a stone vessel for three hours. Then purify it carefully, and dissolve it in Aqua Regis, which is composed of equal parts of vitriol, nitre, and sal ammoniac. Another formula is vitriol, saltpetre, alum, and common salt.

Distil this in an alembic. Pour it on again, and separate carefully the pure from the impure thus. Let it putrefy for a month in horse-dung; then separate the elements in the following manner. If it puts forth its sign1, commence the distillation by means of an alembic with a fire of the first degree. The water and the air will ascend; the fire and the earth will remain at the bottom. Afterwards join them again, and gradually treat with the ashes. So the water and the air will again ascend first, and afterwards the element of fire, which expert artists recognise. The earth will remain in the bottom of the vessel. This collect there. It is what many seek after and few find.

This dead earth in the reverberatory you will prepare according to the rules of Art, and afterwards add fire of the first degree for five days and nights. When these have elapsed you must apply the second degree for the same number of days and nights, and proceed according to Art with the material enclosed. At length you will find a volatile salt, like a thin alkali, containing in itself the Astrum of fire and earth2. Mix this with the two elements that have been preserved, the water and the earth. Again place it on the ashes for eight days and eight nights, and you will find that which has been neglected by many Artists. Separate this according to your experience, and according to the rules of the Spagyric Art, and you will have a white earth, from which its colour has been extracted. Join the element of fire and salt to the alkalised earth. Digest in a pelican to extract the essence. Then a new earth will be deposited, which put aside.

CONCERNING THE RED LION.

Afterwards take the lion in the pelican which also is found [at] first, when you see its tincture, that is to say, the element of fire which stands above the water, the air, and the earth. Separate it from its deposit by trituration. Thus you will have the true aurum potabile$_3$. Sweeten this with the alcohol of wine poured over it, and then distil in an alembic until you perceive no acidity to remain in the Aqua Regia.

This Oil of the Sun, enclosed in a retort hermetically sealed, you must place for elevation that it may be exalted and doubled in its degree. Then put the vessel, still closely shut, in a cool place. Thus it will not be dissolved, but coagulated. Place it again for elevation and coagulation, and repeat this three times. Thus will be produced the Tincture of the Sun, perfect in its degree. Keep this in its own place.

CONCERNING THE GREEN LION.

Take the vitriol of Venus$_4$, carefully prepared according to the rules of Spagyric Art; and add thereto the elements of water and air which you have reserved. Resolve, and set to putrefy for a month according to instructions. When the putrefaction is finished, you will behold the sign of the elements. Separate, and you will soon see two colours, namely, white and red. The red is above the white. The red tincture of the vitriol is so powerful that it reddens all white bodies, and whitens all red ones, which is wonderful.

Work upon this tincture by means of a retort, and you will perceive a blackness issue forth. Treat it again by means of the retort, repeating the operation until it comes out whitish. Go on, and do not despair of the work. Rectify until you find the true, clear Green Lion, which you will recognise by its great weight. You will see that it is heavy and large. This is the Tincture, transparent gold. You will see marvellous signs of this Green Lion, such as could be bought by no treasures of the Roman Leo. Happy he who has learnt how to find it and use it for a tincture!

This is the true and genuine Balsam5, the Balsam of the Heavenly Stars, suffering no bodies to decay, nor allowing leprosy, gout, or dropsy to take root. It is given in a dose of one grain, if it has been fermented with Sulphur of Gold.

Ah, Charles the German, where is your treasure? Where are your philosophers? Where your doctors? Where are your decocters of woods, who at least purge and relax? Is your heaven reversed? Have your stars wandered out of their course, and are they straying in another orbit, away from the line of limitation, since your eyes are smitten with blindness, as by a carbuncle, and other things making a show of ornament, beauty, and pomp? If your artists only knew that their prince Galen - they call none like him - was sticking in hell, from whence he has sent letters to me, they would make the sign of the cross upon themselves with a fox's tail. In the same way your Avicenna sits in the vestibule of the infernal portal; and I have disputed with him about his aurum potabile, his Tincture of the Philosophers, his Quintessence, and Philosophers' Stone, his Mithridatic, his Theriac, and all the rest. O, you hypocrites, who despise the truths taught you by a true physician, who is himself instructed by Nature, and is a son of God himself! Come, then, and listen, impostors who prevail only by the authority of your high positions! After my death, my disciples will burst forth and drag you to the light, and shall expose your dirty drugs, wherewith up to this time you have compassed the death of princes, and the most invincible magnates of the Christian world. Woe for your necks in the day of judgment! I know that the monarchy will be mine. Mine, too, will be the honour and glory. Not that I praise myself: Nature praises me. Of her I am born; her I follow. She knows me, and I know her. The light which is in her I have beheld in her; outside, too, I have proved the same in the figure of the microcosm, and found it in that universe.

But I must proceed with my design in order to satisfy my disciples to the full extent of their wish. I willingly do this for them, if only skilled in the light of Nature and thoroughly practised in astral matters, they finally become adepts in philosophy, which enables them to know the nature of every kind of water.

Take, then, of this liquid of the minerals which I have described, four parts by weight; of the Earth of red Sol two parts; of Sulphur of Sol one part. Put these together into a pelican, congelate, and dissolve them three times. Thus you will have the Tincture of the Alchemists. We have not here described its weight: but this is given in the book on Transmutations6.

So, now, he who has one to a thousand ounces of the Astrum Solis shall also tinge his own body of Sol.

If you have the Astrum of Mercury, in the same manner, you will tinge the whole body of common Mercury. If you have the Astrum of Venus you will, in like manner, tinge the whole body of Venus, and change it into the best metal. These facts have all been proved. The same must also be understood as to the Astra of the other planets, as Saturn, Jupiter, Mars, Luna, and the rest. For tinctures are also prepared from these: concerning which we now make no mention in this place, because we have already dwelt at sufficient length upon them in the book on the Nature of Things and in the Archidoxies. So, too, the first entity of metals and terrestrial minerals have been made, sufficiently clear for Alchemists to enable them to get the Alchemists' Tincture.

This work, the Tincture of the Alchemists, need not be one of nine months; but quickly, and without any delay, you may go on by the Spaygric Art of the Alchemists, and, in the space of forty days, you can fix this alchemical substance, exalt it, putrefy it, ferment it, coagulate it into a stone, and produce the Alchemical Phoenix7. But it should be noted well that the Sulphur of Cinnabar becomes the Flying Eagle, whose wings fly away without wind, and carry the body of the phoenix to the nest of the parent, where it is nourished by the element of fire, and the young ones dig out its eyes: from whence there emerges a whiteness, divided in its sphere, into a sphere and life out of its own heart, by the balsam of its inward parts, according to the property of the cabalists.

HERE ENDS THE TREASURE OF THE ALCHEMISTS.

NOTES

1 The *Sign* is nothing else than the mark left by an operation. The house constructed by the architect is the sign of his handicraft whereby his skill and art are determined. Thus the sign is the achievement itself. - *De Colica.*

2 The earth also has its Astrum, its course, its order, just as much as the Firmament, but peculiar to the element. So also there is an Astrum in the water, even as in the earth, and in like manner with air and fire. Consequently, the upper Astrum has the Astra of the elements for its medium and operates through them by an irresistible attraction. Through this operation of the superior and inferior Astra, all things are fecundated, and led on to their end. - *Explicatio Totius Astronomiae.* Without the Astra the elements cannot flourish. ... In the Astrum of the earth all the celestial operations thrive. The Astrum itself is hidden, the bodies are manifest. ... The motion of the earth is brought about by the Astrum of the earth. ... There are four Astra in man (corresponding to those of the four elements), for he is the lesser world. - *De Caducis,* Par. II.

3 *Aurum Potabile,* that is, Potable Gold, Oil of Gold, and Quintessence of Gold, are distinguished thus. *Aurum Potabile* is gold rendered potable by intermixture with other substances, and with liquids. Oil of Gold is an oil extracted from the precious metal without the addition of anything. The Quintessence of Gold is the redness of gold extracted therefrom and separated from the body of the metal. - *De Membris Contractis,* Tract II., c. 2.

4 If copper be pounded and resolved without a corrosive, you have Vitriol. From this may be prepared the quintessence, oil, and liquor thereof. - *De Morbis Tartareis.* Cuprine Vitriol is Vitriol cooked with Copper. - *De Morbis Vermium,* Par. 6. Chalcanthum is present in Venus, and Venus can by separation be reduced into Chalcanthum. - *Chirurgia Magna.* Pars. III., Lib. IV.

5 There is, indeed, diffused through all things a Balsam created by God, without which putrefaction would immediately supervene. Thus in corpses which are anointed with Balsam we see that corruption is arrested and thus in the physical body we infer that there is a certain natural and congenital Balsam, in the absence of which the living and complete man would not be safe from putrefaction. Nothing removes the Balsam but death. But this kind differs from what is more commonly called Balsam, in that the one is conservative of the living, and the other of the dead. - *Chirurgia Magna*, Pt. II., Tract II., c 3. The confection of Balsam requires special knowledge of chemistry, and it was first discovered by the Alchemists. - *Ibid.*, Pt. I., Tract II., c. 4.

6 It is difficult to identify the treatise to which reference is made here. It does not seem to be the seventh book concerning The Nature of Things, nor the ensuing tract on Cements. The general question of natural and artificial weight is discussed in the *Aurora of the Philosophers*. No detached work on Transmutations has come down to us.

7 Know that the Phoenix is the soul of the Iliaster (that is, the first chaos of the matter of all things). ... It is also the Iliastic soul in man. - *Liber Azoth*, S. V., *Practica Lineae Vitae*.

THE AURORA OF THE PHILOSOPHERS.

THE AURORA OF THE PHILOSOPHERS.

THEOPHRASTUS PARACELSUS.

WHICH HE OTHERWISE CALLS HIS MONARCHIA.[1]

CHAPTER I.

CONCERNING THE ORIGIN OF THE PHILOSOPHERS' STONE.

Adam was the first inventor of arts, because he had knowledge of all things as well after the Fall as before[2]. Thence he predicted the world's destruction by water. From this cause, too, it came about that his successors erected two tables of stone, on which they engraved all natural arts in hieroglyphical characters, in order that their posterity might also become acquainted with this prediction, that so it might be heeded, and provision made in the time of danger. Subsequently, Noah found one of these tables under Mount Araroth, after the Deluge. In this table were described the courses of the upper firmament and of the lower globe, and also of the planets. At length this universal knowledge was divided into several parts, and lessened in its vigour and power. By means of this separation, one man became an astronomer, another a magician, another a cabalist, and a fourth an alchemist. Abraham, that Vulcanic Tubalcain, a consummate astrologer and arithmetician, carried the Art out of the land of Canaan into Egypt, whereupon the Egyptians rose to so great a height and dignity that this wisdom was derived from them by other nations. The patriarch Jacob painted, as it were, the sheep with various colours; and this was done by magic: for in the theology of the Chaldeans, Hebrews, Persians, and Egyptians, they held these arts to be the highest philosophy, to be learnt by their chief nobles and priests. So it was in the time of Moses, when both the priests and also the physicians were chosen from among the Magi – the priests for the judgment of what related to health, especially in the knowledge of leprosy. Moses, likewise, was instructed in the Egyptian schools, at the cost and care of Pharaoh's daughter, so that he excelled in all the wisdom and learning of that people. Thus, too, was it with Daniel, who in his youthful days imbibed the learning of the Chaldeans, so that he became a cabalist. Witness his divine predictions and his exposition of those words, "Mene, Mene, Tecelphares". These words can be understood by the prophetic and cabalistic Art. This cabalistic Art was perfectly familiar to, and in constant use by, Moses and the Prophets. The Prophet Elias foretold many things by his cabalistic numbers. So did the Wise Men of old, by this natural and mystical Art, learn to know God rightly. They abode in His laws, and walked in His statutes with great firmness. It is also evident in the Book of Samuel, that the Berelists did not follow the devil's part, but became, by Divine permission, partakers of visions and veritable apparitions, whereof we shall treat more at large in the Book of Supercelestial Things[3]. This gift is granted by the Lord God to those priests who walk in the Divine precepts. It was a custom among the Persians never to admit any one as king unless he were a Wise Man, pre-eminent in reality as well as in name. This is clear from the customary name of their kings; for they were called Wise Men. Such were those Wise Men and Persian Magi who came from the East to seek out the Lord Jesus, and are called natural priests. The Egyptians, also, having obtained this magic and philosophy from the Chaldeans and Persians, desired that their priests should learn the same wisdom; and they became so fruitful and successful therein that all the neighbouring countries admired them. For this reason Hermes was so truly named Trismegistus, because he was a king, a priest, a prophet, a magician, and a sophist of natural things. Such another was Zoroaster.

CHAPTER II.

WHEREIN IS DECLARED THAT THE GREEKS DREW A LARGE PART OF THEIR LEARNING FROM THE EGYPTIANS; AND HOW IT CAME FROM THEM TO US.

When a son of Noah possessed the third part of the world after the Flood, this Art broke into Chaldaea and Persia, and thence spread into Egypt. The Art having been found out by the superstitious and idolatrous Greeks, some of them who were wiser than the rest betook themselves to the Chaldeans and Egyptians, so that they might draw the same wisdom from their schools. Since, however, the theological study of the law of Moses did not satisfy them, they trusted to their own peculiar genius, and fell away from the right foundation of those natural secrets and arts. This is evident from their fabulous conceptions, and from their errors respecting the doctrine of Moses. It was the custom of the Egyptians to put forward the traditions of that surpassing wisdom only in enigmatical figures and abstruse histories and terms. This was afterwards followed by Homer with marvellous poetical skill; and Pythagoras was also acquainted with it, seeing that he comprised in his writings many things out of the law of Moses and the Old Testament. In like manner, Hippocrates, Thales of Miletus, Anaxagoras, Democritus, and others, did not scruple to fix their minds on the same subject. And yet none of them were practised in the true Astrology, Geometry, Arithmetic, or Medicine, because their pride prevented this, since they would not admit disciples belonging to other nations than their own. Even when they had got some insight from the Chaldeans and Egyptians, they became more arrogant still than they were before by Nature, and without any diffidence propounded the subject substantially indeed, but mixed with subtle fictions or falsehoods; and then they attempted to elaborate a certain kind of philosophy which descended from them to the Latins. These in their turn, being educated herewith, adorned it with their own doctrines, and by these the philosophy was spread over Europe. Many academies were founded for the propagation of their dogmas and rules, so that the young might be instructed; and this system flourishes with the Germans, and other nations, right down to the present day.

CHAPTER III.

WHAT WAS TAUGHT IN THE SCHOOLS OF THE EGYPTIANS.

The Chaldeans, Persians, and Egyptians had all of them the same knowledge of the secrets of Nature, and also the same religion. It was only the names that differed. The Chaldeans and Persians called their doctrine Sophia and Magic[4]; and the Egyptians, because of the sacrifice, called their wisdom priestcraft. The magic of the Persians, and the theology of the Egyptians, were both of them taught in the schools of old. Though there were many schools and learned men in Arabia, Africa, and Greece, such as Albumazar, Abenzagel, Geber, Rhasis, and Avicenna among the Arabians; and among the Greeks, Machaon, Podalirius, Pythagoras, Anaxagoras, Democritus, Plato, Aristotle, and Rhodianus; still there were different opinions amongst them as to the wisdom of the Egyptian on points wherein they themselves differed, and whereupon they disagreed with it. For this reason Pythagoras could not be called a wise man, because the Egyptian priestcraft and wisdom were not perpectly taught, although he received therefrom many mysteries and arcana; and that Anaxagoras had received a great many as well, is clear from his discussions on the subject of Sol and its Stone, which he left behind him after his death. Yet he differed in many respects from the Egyptians. Even they would not be called wise men or Magi; but, following Pythagoras, they assumed the name of philosophy: yet they gathered no more than a few gleams like shadows from the magic of the Persians and the Egyptians. But Moses, Abraham, Solomon, Adam, and the wise men that came from the East to

Christ, were true Magi, divine sophists and cabalists. Of this art and wisdom the Greeks knew very little or nothing at all; and therefore we shall leave this philosophical wisdom of the Greeks as being a mere speculation, utterly distinct and separate from other true arts and sciences.

CHAPTER IV.

WHAT MAGI THE CHALDEANS, PERSIANS, AND EGYPTIANS WERE.

Many persons have endeavoured to investigate and make use of the secret magic of these wise men; but it has not yet been accomplished. Many even of our own age exalt Trithemius, others Bacon and Agrippa, for magic and the cabala[5] – two things apparently quite distinct – not knowing why they do so. Magic, indeed, is an art and faculty whereby the elementary bodies, their fruits, properties, virtues, and hidden operations are comprehended. But the cabala, by a subtle understanding of the Scriptures, seems to trace out the way to God for men, to shew them how they may act with Him, and prophesy from Him; for the cabala is full of divine mysteries, even as Magic is full of natural secrets. It teaches of and foretells from the nature of things to come as well as of things present, since its operation consists in knowing the inner constitution of all creatures, of celestial as well as terrestrial bodies: what is latent within them; what are their occult virtues; for what they were originally designed, and with what properties they are endowed. These and the like subjects are the bonds wherewith things celestial are bound up with things of the earth, as may sometimes be seen in their operation even with the bodily eyes. Such a conjunction of celestial influences, whereby the heavenly virtues acted upon inferior bodies, was formerly called by the Magi a Gamahea[6], or the marriage of the celestial powers and properties with elementary bodies. Hence ensued the excellent commixtures of all bodies, celestial and terrestrial, namely, of the sun and planets, likewise vegetables, minerals, and animals.

The devil attempted with his whole force and endeavour to darken this light; nor was he wholly frustrated in his hopes, for he deprived all Greece of it, and, in place thereof, introduced among that people human speculations and simple blasphemies against God and against His Son. Magic, it is true, had its origin in the Divine Ternary and arose from the Trinity of God. For God marked all His creatures with this Ternary and engraved its hieroglyph on them with His own finger. Nothing in the nature of things can be assigned or produced that lacks this magistery of the Divine Ternary, or that does not even ocularly prove it. The creature teaches us to understand and see the Creator Himself, as St. Paul testifies to the Romans. This covenant of the Divine Ternary, diffused throughout the whole substance of things, is indissoluble. By this, also, we have the secrets of all Nature from the four elements. For the Ternary, with the magical Quaternary, produces a perfect Septenary, endowed with many arcana and demonstrated by things which are known. When the Quaternary rests in the Ternary, then arises the Light of the World on the horizon of eternity, and by the assistance of God gives us the whole bond. Here also it refers to the virtues and operations of all creatures, and to their use, since they are stamped and marked with their arcana, signs, characters, and figures, so that there is left in them scarcely the smallest occult point which is not made clear on examination. Then when the Quaternary and the Ternary mount to the Denary is accomplished their retrogression or reduction to unity. Herein is comprised all the occult wisdom of things which God has made plainly manifest to men, both by His word and by the creatures of His hands, so that they may have a true knowledge of them. This shall be made more clear in another place.

CHAPTER V.

CONCERNING THE CHIEF AND SUPREME ESSENCE OF THINGS.

The Magi in their wisdom asserted that all creatures might be brought to one unified substance, which substance they affirm may, by purifications and purgations, attain to so high a degree of subtlety, such divine nature and occult property, as to work wonderful results. For they considered that by returning to the earth, and by a supreme magical separation, a certain perfect substance would come forth, which is at length, by many industrious and prolonged preparations, exalted and raised up above the range of vegetable substances into mineral, above mineral into metallic, and above perfect metallic substances into a perpetual and divine Quintessence[7], including in itself the essence of all celestial and terrestrial creatures. The Arabs and Greeks, by the occult characters and hieroglyphic descriptions of the Persians and the Egyptians, attained to secret and abstruse mysteries. When these were obtained and partially understood they saw with their own eyes, in the course of experimenting, many wonderful and strange effects. But since the supercelestial operations lay more deeply hidden than their capacity could penetrate, they did not call this a supercelestial arcanum according to the institution of the Magi, but the arcanum of the Philosophers' Stone according to the counsel and judgment of Pythagoras. Whoever obtained this Stone overshadowed it with various enigmatical figures, deceptive resemblances, comparisons, and fictitious titles, so that its matter might remain occult. Very little or no knowledge of it therefore can be had from them.

CHAPTER VI.

CONCERNING THE DIFFERENT ERRORS AS TO ITS DISCOVERY AND KNOWLEDGE.

The philosophers have prefixed most occult names to this matter of the Stone, grounded on mere similitudes. Arnold, observing this, says in his "Rosary" that the greatest difficulty is to find out the material of this Stone; for they have called it vegetable, animal, and mineral, but not according to the literal sense, which is well known to such wise men as have had experience of divine secrets and the miracles of this same Stone. For example, Raymond Lully's "Lunaria" may be cited. This gives flowers of admirable virtues familiar to the philosophers themselves; but it was not the intention of those philosophers that you should think they meant thereby any projection upon metals, or that any such preparations should be made; but the abstruse mind of the philosophers had another intention. In like manner, they called their matter by the name of Martagon, to which they applied an occult alchemical operation; when, notwithstanding that name, it denotes nothing more than a hidden similitude. Moreover, no small error has arisen in the liquid of vegetables, with which a good many have sought to coagulate Mercury[8], and afterwards to convert it with fixatory waters into Luna, since they supposed that he who in this way could coagulate it without the aid of metals would succeed in becoming the chief master. Now, although the liquids of some vegetables do effect this, yet the result is due merely to the resin, fat, and earthy sulphur with which they abound. This attracts to itself the moisture of the Mercury which rises with the substance in the process of coagulation, but without any advantage resulting. I am well assured that no thick and external Sulphur in vegetables is adapted for a perfect projection in Alchemy, as some have found out to their cost. Certain persons have, it is true, coagulated Mercury with the white and milky juice of tittinal, on account of the intense heat which exists therein; and they have called that liquid "Lac Virginis"; yet this is a false basis. The same may be asserted concerning the juice of celandine, although it colours just as though it were endowed with gold. Hence people conceived a vain idea. At a certain fixed time they rooted up this vegetable, from which they sought for a soul or quintessence, wherefrom they might make a coagulating and transmuting tincture. But hence arose nothing save a foolish error.

CHAPTER VII.

CONCERNING THE ERRORS OF THOSE WHO SEEK THE
STONE IN VEGETABLES.

Some alchemists have pressed a juice out of celandine, boiled it to thickness, and put it in the sun, so that it might coagulate into a hard mass, which, being afterwards pounded into a fine black powder, should turn Mercury by projection into Sol. This they also found to be in vain. Others mixed Sal Ammoniac with this powder; others the Colcothar of Vitriol, supposing that they would thus arrive at their desired result. They brought it by their solutions into a yellow water, so that the Sal Ammoniac allowed an entrance of the tincture into the substance of the Mercury. Yet again nothing was accomplished. There are some again who, instead of the abovementioned substances, take the juices of persicaria, bufonaria, dracunculus, the leaves of willow, tithymal, cataputia, flammula, and the like, and shut them up in a glass vessel with Mercury for some days, keeping them in ashes. Thus it comes about that the Mercury is turned into ashes, but deceptively and without any result. These people were misled by the vain rumours of the vulgar, who give it out that he who is able to coagulate Mercury without metals has the entire Magistery, as we have said before. Many, too, have extracted salts, oils, and sulphurs artificially out of vegetables, but quite in vain. Out of such salts, oils, and sulphurs no coagulation of Mercury, or perfect projection, or tincture, can be made. But when the philosophers compare their matter to a certain golden tree of seven boughs, they mean that such matter includes all the seven metals in its sperm, and that in it these lie hidden. On this account they called their matter vegetable, because, as in the case of natural trees, they also in their time produce various flowers. So, too, the matter of the Stone shews most beautiful colours in the production of its flowers. The comparison, also, is apt, because a certain matter rises out of the philosophical earth, as if it were a thicket of branches and sprouts: like a sponge growing on the earth. They say, therefore, that the fruit of their tree tends towards heaven. So, then, they put forth that the whole thing hinged upon natural vegetables, though not as to its matter, because their stone contains within itself a body, soul, and spirit, as vegetables do.

CHAPTER VIII.

CONCERNING THOSE WHO HAVE SOUGHT THE STONE IN ANIMALS.

They have also, by a name based only on resemblances, called this matter Lac Virginis, and the Blessed Blood of Rosy Colour, which, nevertheless, suits only the prophets and sons of God. Hence the sophists[9] gathered that this philosophical matter was in the blood of animals or of man. Sometimes, too, because they are nourished by vegetables, others have sought it in hairs, in salt of urine, in rebis; others in hens' eggs, in milk, and in the calx of egg shells, with all of which they thought they would be able to fix Mercury. Some have extracted salt out of foetid urine, supposing that to be the matter of the Stone. Some persons, again, have considered the little stones found in rebis to be the matter. Others have macerated the membranes of eggs in a sharp lixivium, with which they also mixed calcined egg shells as white as snow. To these they have attributed the arcanum of fixation for the transmutation of Mercury. Others, comparing the white of the egg to silver and the yolk to gold, have chosen it for their matter, mixing with it common salt, sal ammoniac, and burnt tartar. These they shut up in a glass vessel, and puri6ed in a *Balneum Maris* until the white matter became as red as blood. This, again, they distilled into a most offensive liquid, utterly useless for the purpose they had in view. Others have purified the white and yolk of eggs; from which has been generated a basilisk. This they burnt to a deep red powder, and sought to tinge with it, as they learnt from the treatise of Cardinal Gilbert. Many, again, have macerated the galls of oxen, mixed with common salt, and distilled this into a liquid, with which they moistened the cementary powders, supposing that, by means of this Magistery, they would tinge their metals. This they called by the name of "a part with a part", and thence came – just nothing. Others have attempted to transmute tutia by the addition of dragon's blood and other substances, and also to change copper and electrum into gold. Others, according to the Venetian Art, as they call it, take twenty lizard-like animals, more or less, shut them up in a vessel, and make them mad with hunger, so that they may devour one another until only one of them survives. This one is then fed with filings of copper or of electrum. They suppose that this animal, simply by the digestion of his stomach, will bring about the desired transmutation. Finally, they burn this animal into a red powder, which they thought must be gold; but they were deceived. Others, again, having burned the fishes called truitas (? trouts), have sometimes, upon melting them, found some gold in them; but there is no other reason for it than this: Those fish sometimes in rivers and streams meet with certain small scales and sparks of gold, which they eat. It is seldom, however, that such deceivers are found, and then chiefly in the courts of princes. The matter of the philosophers is not to be sought in animals: this I announce to all. Still, it is evident that the philosophers called their Stone animal, because in their final operations the virtue of this most excellent fiery mystery caused an obscure liquid to exude drop by drop from the matter in their vessels. Hence they predicted that, in the last times, there should come a most pure man upon the earth, by whom the redemption of the world should be brought about; and that this man should send forth bloody drops of a red colour, by means of which he should redeem the world from sin. In the same way, after its own kind, the blood of their Stone freed the leprous metals from their infirmities and contagion. On these grounds, therefore, they supposed they were justified in saying that their Stone was animal. Concerning this mystery Mercurius speaks as follows to King Calid: –

"This mystery it is permitted only to the prophets of God to know. Hence it comes to pass that this Stone is called animal, because in its blood a soul lies hid. It is likewise composed of body, spirit, and soul. For the same reason they called it their microcosm, because it has the likeness of all things in the world, and thence they termed it animal, as Plato named the great world an animal".

CHAPTER IX.

CONCERNING THOSE WHO HAVE SOUGHT THE STONE IN MINERALS.

Hereto are added the many ignorant men who suppose the stone to be three-fold, and to be hidden in a triple genus, namely, vegetable, animal, and mineral. Hence it is that they have sought for it in minerals. Now, this is far from the opinion of the philosophers. They affirm that their stone is uniformly vegetable, animal, and mineral. Now, here note that Nature has distributed its mineral sperm into various kinds, as, for instance, into sulphurs, salts, boraxes, nitres, ammoniacs, alums, arsenics, atraments, vitriols, tutias, haematites, orpiments, realgars, magnesias, cinnabar, antimony, talc, cachymia, marcasites, etc. In all these Nature has not yet attained to our matter; although in some of the species named it displays itself in a wonderful aspect for the transmutation of imperfect metals that are to be brought to perfection. Truly, long experience and practice with fire shew many and various permutations in the matter of minerals, not only from one colour to another, but from one essence to another, and from imperfection to perfection. And, although Nature has, by means of prepared minerals, reached some perfection, yet philosophers will not have it that the matter of the philosophic stone proceeds out of any of the minerals, although they say that their stone is universal. Hence, then, the sophists take occasion to persecute Mercury himself with various torments, as with sublimations, coagulations, mercurial waters, aquafortis, and the like. All these erroneous ways should be avoided, together with other sophistical preparations of minerals, and the purgations and fixations of spirits and metals. Wherefore all the preparations of the stone, as of Geber, Albertus Magnus, and the rest, are sophistical. Their purgations, cementations, sublimations, distillations, rectifications, circulations, putrefactions, conjunctions, solutions, ascensions, coagulations, calcinations, and incinerations are utterly profitless, both in the tripod, in the athanor, in the reverberatory furnace, in the melting furnace, the accidioneum, in dung, ashes, sand, or what not; and also in the cucurbite, the pelican, retort, phial, fixatory, and the rest. The same opinion must be passed on the sublimation of Mercury by mineral spirits, for the white and the red, as by vitriol, saltpetre, alum, crocuses, etc., concerning all which subjects that sophist, John de Rupescissa, romances in his treatise on the White and Red Philosophic Stone. Taken altogether, these are merely deceitful dreams. Avoid also the particular sophistry of Geber; for example, his sevenfold sublimations or mortifications, and also the revivifications of Mercury, with his preparations of salts of urine, or salts made by a sepulchre, all which things are untrustworthy. Some others have endeavoured to fix Mercury with: the sulphurs of minerals and metals, but have been greatly deceived. It is true I have seen Mercury by this Art, and by such fixations, brought into a metallic body resembling and counterfeiting good silver in all respects; but when brought to the test it has shewn itself to be false.

CHAPTER X.

CONCERNING THOSE WHO HAVE SOUGHT THE STONE AND ALSO PARTICULARS IN MINERALS.

Some sophists have tried to squeeze out a fixed oil from Mercury seven times sublimed and as often dissolved by means of aquafortis. In this way they attempt to bring imperfect metals to perfection: but they have been obliged to relinquish their vain endeavour. Some have purged vitriol seven times by calcination, solution, and coagulation, with the addition of two parts of sal ammoniac, and by sublimation, so that it might be resolved into a white water, to which they have added a third part of quicksilver, that it might be coagulated by water. Then afterwards they have sublimated the Mercury several times from the vitriol and sal ammoniac, so that it became a stone. This stone they affirmed, being conceived of the vitriol, to be the Red Sulphur of the philosophers, with which they have, by means of solutions and coagulations, made some progress in attaining the stone; but in projection it has all come to nothing. Others have coagulated Mercury by water of alum into a hard mass like alum itself; and this they have fruitlessly fixed with fixatory waters. The sophists propose to themselves very many ways of fixing Mercury, but to no purpose, for therein nothing perfect or constant can be had. It is therefore in vain to add minerals thereto by sophistical processes, since by all of them he is stirred up to greater malice, is rendered more lively, and rather brought to greater impurity than to any kind of perfection. So, then, the philosophers' matter is not to be sought from thence. Mercury is somewhat imperfect; and to bring it to perfection will be very difficult, nay, impossible for any sophist. There is nothing therein that can be stirred up or compelled to perfection. Some have taken arsenic several times sublimated, and frequently dissolved with oil of tartar and coagulated. This they have pretended to fix, and by it to turn copper into silver. This, however, is merely a sophistical whitening, for arsenic cannot be fixed[10] unless the operator be an Artist, and knows well its tingeing spirit. Truly in this respect all the philosophers have slept, vainly attempting to accomplish anything thereby. Whoever, therefore, is ignorant as to this spirit, cannot have any hopes of fixing it, or of giving it that power which would make it capable of the virtue of transmutation. So, then, I give notice to all that the whitening of which I have just now spoken is grounded on a false basis, and that by it the copper is deceitfully whitened, but not changed.

Now the sophists have mixed this counterfeit Venus with twice its weight of Luna, and sold it to the goldsmiths and mint-masters, until at last they have transmuted themselves into false coiners – not only those who sold, but those who bought it. Some sophists instead of white arsenic take red, and this has turned out false art; because, however it is prepared, it proves to be nothing but whiteness.

Some, again, have gone further and dealt with common sulphur, which, being so yellow, they have boiled in vinegar, lixivium, or sharpest wines, for a day and a night, until it became white. Then afterwards they sublimated it from common salt and the calx of eggs, repeating the process several times; yet, still, though white, it has been always combustible. Nevertheless, with this they have endeavoured to fix Mercury and to turn it into gold; but in vain. From this, however, comes the most excellent and beautiful cinnabar that I have ever seen. This they propose to fix with the oil of sulphur by cementation and fixation. It does, indeed, give something of an appearance, but still falls short of the desired object. Others have reduced common sulphur to the form of a hepar, boiling it in vinegar with the addition of linseed oil, or laterine oil, or olive oil. They then pour it into a marble mortar, and make it into the form of a hepar, which they have first distilled into a citrine oil with a gentle fire. But they have found to their loss that they could not do anything in the way of transmuting Luna to Sol as they supposed they would be able. As there is an infinite number of metals, so also there is much variety in the preparation of them: I shall not make further mention of these in this place, because each a mould require a special treatise. Beware also of sophisticated oils of vitriol and antimony. Likewise be on your guard against the oils of the metals, perfect or imperfect, as Sol or Luna; because although the operation of these is most potent in the nature of things, yet the true process is known, even at this day, to very few persons. Abstain also from the sophistical preparations of common mercury, arsenic, sulphur, and the like, by sublimation, descension, fixation by vinegar, saltpetre, tartar, vitriol, sal ammoniac, according to the formulas prescribed in the books of the sophists. Likewise avoid the sophisticated tinctures taken from marcasites and crocus of Mars, and also of that sophistication called by the name of "a part with a part", and of fixed Luna and similar trifles. Although they have some superficial appearance of truth, as the fixation of Luna by little labour and industry, still the progress of the preparation is worthless and weak. Being therefore moved with compassion towards the well meaning operators in this art, I have determined to lay open the whole foundation of philosophy in three separate arcana, namely, in one explained by arsenic, in a second by vitriol, and in a third by antimony; by means of which I will teach the true projection upon Mercury and upon the imperfect metals.

CHAPTER XI.

CONCERNING THE TRUE AND PERFECT SPECIAL ARCANUM OF ARSENIC FOR THE WHITE TINCTURE.

Some persons have written that arsenic is compounded of Mercury and, Sulphur, others of earth and water; but most writers say that it is of the nature of Sulphur. But, however that may be, its nature is such that it transmutes red copper into white. It may also be brought to such a perfect state of preparation as to be able to tinge. But this is not done in the way pointed out by such evil sophists as Geber in "The Sum of Perfection", Albertus Magnus, Aristotle the chemist in "The Book of the Perfect Magistery", Rhasis and Polydorus; for those writers, however many they be, are either themselves in error, or else they write falsely out of sheer envy, and put forth receipts whilst not ignorant of the truth. Arsenic contains within itself three natural spirits. The first is volatile, combustible, corrosive, and penetrating all metals. This spirit whitens Venus and after some days renders it spongy. But this artifice relates only to those who practise the caustic art. The second spirit is crystalline and sweet. The third is a tingeing spirit separated from the others before mentioned. True philosophers seek for these three natural properties in arsenic with a view to the perfect projection of the wise men[11]. But those barbers who practise surgery seek after that sweet and crystalline nature separated from the tingeing spirit for use in the cure of wounds, buboes, carbuncles, anthrax, and other similar ulcers which are not curable save by gentle means. As for that tingeing spirit, however, unless the pure be separated from the impure in it, the fixed from the volatile, and the secret tincture from the combustible, it will not in any way succeed according to your wish for projection on Mercury, Venus, or any other imperfect metal. All philosophers have hidden this arcanum as a most excellent mystery. This tingeing spirit, separated from the other two as above, you must join to the spirit of Luna, and digest them together for the space of thirty-two days, or until they have assumed a new body. After it has, on the fortieth natural day, been kindled into flame by the heat of the sun, the spirit appears in a bright whiteness, and is endued with a perfect tingeing arcanum. Then it is at length fit for projection, namely, one part of it upon sixteen parts of an imperfect body, according to the sharpness of the preparation. From thence appears shining and most excellent Luna, as though it had been dug from the bowels of the earth.

CHAPTER XII.

GENERAL INSTRUCTION CONCERNING THE ARCANUM OF VITRIOL AND

THE RED TINCTURE TO BE EXTRACTED FROM IT.[12]

Vitriol is a very noble mineral among the rest, and was held always in highest estimation by philosophers, because the Most High God has adorned it with wonderful gifts. They have veiled its arcanum in enigmatical figures like the following: "Thou shalt go to the inner parts of the earth, and by rectification thou shalt find the occult stone, a true medicine". By the earth they understood the Vitriol itself; and by the inner parts of the earth its sweetness and redness, because in the occult part of the Vitriol lies hid a subtle, noble, and most fragrant juice, and a pure oil. The method of its production is not to be approached by calcination or by distillation. For it must not be deprived on any account of its green colour. If it were, it would at the same time lose its arcanum and its power. Indeed, it should be observed at this point that minerals, and also vegetables and other like things which shew greenness without, contain within themselves an oil red like blood, which is their arcanum. Hence it is clear that the distillations of the druggists are useless, vain, foolish, and of no value, because these people do not know how to extract the bloodlike redness from vegetables. Nature herself is wise, and turns all the waters of vegetables to a lemon colour, and after that into an oil which is very red like blood. The reason why this is so slowly accomplished arises from the too great haste of the ignorant operators who distil it, which causes the greenness to be consumed. They have not learnt to strengthen Nature with their own powers, which is the mode whereby that noble green colour ought to be rectified into redness of itself. An example of this is white wine digesting itself into a lemon colour; and in process of time the green colour of the grape is of itself turned into the red which underlies the coerulean. The greenness therefore of the vegetables and minerals being lost by the incapacity of the operators, the essence also and spirit of the oil and of the balsam, which is noblest among arcana, will also perish.

CHAPTER XIII.

SPECIAL INSTRUCTION CONCERNING THE PROCESS OF VITRIOL FOR THE RED TINCTURE.

Vitriol contains within itself many muddy and viscous imperfections. Therefore its greenness[13] must be often extracted with water, and rectified until it puts off all the impurities of earth. When all these rectifications are finished, take care above all that the matter shall not be exposed to the sun, for this turns its greenness pale, and at the same time absorbs the arcanum. Let it be kept covered up in a warm stove so that no dust may defile it. Afterwards let it be digested in a closed glass vessel for the space of several months, or until different colours and deep redness shew themselves. Still you must not suppose that by this process the redness is sufficiently fixed. It must, in addition, be cleansed from the interior and accidental defilements of the earth, in the following manner: – It must be rectified with acetum until the earthy defilement is altogether removed, and the dregs are taken away. This is now the true and best rectification of its tincture, from which the blessed oil is to be extracted. From this tincture, which is carefully enclosed in a glass vessel, an alembic afterwards placed on it and luted so that no spirit may escape, the spirit of this oil must be extracted by distillation over a mild and slow fire. This oil is much pleasanter and sweeter than any aromatic balsam of the drugsellers, being entirely free from all acridity[14]. There will subside in tha bottom of the cucurbite some very white earth, shining and glittering like snow. This keep, and protect from all dust. This same earth is altogether separated from its redness.

Thereupon follows the greatest arcanum, that is to say, the Supercelestial Marriage of the Soul, consummately prepared and washed by the blood of the lamb, with its own splendid, shining, and purified body. This is the true supercelestial marriage by which life is prolonged to the last and predestined day. In this way, then, the soul and spirit of the Vitriol, which are its blood, are joined with its purified body, that they may be for eternity inseparable. Take, therefore, this our foliated earth in a glass phial. Into it pour gradually its own oil. The body will receive and embrace its soul; since the body is affected with extreme desire for the soul, and the soul is most perfectly delighted with the embrace of the body. Place this conjunction in a furnace of arcana, and keep it there for forty days. When these have expired you will have a most absolute oil of wondrous perfection, in which Mercury and any other of the imperfect metals are turned into gold.

Now let us turn our attention to its multiplication. Take the corporal Mercury, in the proportion of two parts; pour it over three parts, equal in weight, of the aforesaid oil, and let them remain together for forty days. By this proportion of weight and this order the multiplication becomes infinite.

CHAPTER XIV.

CONCERNING THE SECRETS AND ARCANA OF ANTIMONY, FOR THE RED TINCTURE, WITH A VIEW TO TRANSMUTATION.

Antimony is the true bath of gold. Philosophers call it the examiner and the stilanx. Poets say that in this bath Vulcan washed Phoebus, and purified him from all dirt and imperfection. It is produced from the purest and noblest Mercury and Sulphur, under the genus of vitriol, in metallic form and brightness. Some philosophers call it the White Lead of the Wise Men, or simply the Lead. Take, therefore, of Antimony, the very best of its kind, as much as you will. Dissolve this in its own aquafortis, and throw it into cold water, adding a little of the crocus of Mars, so that it may sink to the bottom of the vessel as a sediment, for otherwise it does not throw off its dregs. After it has been dissolved in this way it will have acquired supreme beauty. Let it be placed in a glass vessel, closely fastened on all sides with a very thick lute, or else in a stone bocia, and mix with it some calcined tutia, sublimated to the perfect degree of fire. It must be carefully guarded from liquefying, because with too great heat it breaks the glass. From one pound of this Antimony a sublimation is made, perfected for a space of two days. Place this sublimated substance in a phial that it may touch the water with its third part, in a luted vessel, so that the spirit may not escape. Let it be suspended over the tripod of arcana, and let the work be urged on at first with a slow fire equal to the sun's heat at midsummer. Then at length on the tenth day let it be gradually increased. For with too great heat the glass vessels are broken, and sometimes even the furnace goes to pieces. While the vapour is ascending different colours appear. Let the fire be moderated until a red matter is seen. Afterwards dissolve in very sharp Acetum, and throw away the dregs. Let the Acetum be abstracted and let it be again dissolved in common distilled water. This again must be abstracted, and the sediment distilled with a very strong fire in a glass vessel closely shut. The whole body of the Antimony will ascend as a very red oil, like the colour of a ruby, and will flow into the receiver, drop by drop, with a most fragrant smell and a very sweet taste[15]. This is the supreme arcanum of the philosophers in Antimony, which they account most highly among the arcana of oils. Then, lastly, let the oil of Sol be made in the following way: – Take of the purest Sol as much as you will, and dissolve it in rectified spirit of wine. Let the spirit be abstracted several times, and an equal number of times let it be dissolved again. Let the last solution be kept with the spirit of wine, and circulated for a month. Afterwards let the volatile gold and the spirit of wine be distilled three or four times by means of an alembic, so that it may flow down into the receiver and be brought to its supreme essence. To half an ounce of this dissolved gold let one ounce of the Oil of Antimony be added. This oil embraces it in the heat of the bath, so that it does not easily let it go, even if the spirit of wine be extracted. In this way you will have the supreme mystery and arcanum of Nature, to which scarcely any equal can be assigned in the nature of things. Let these two oils in combination be shut up together in a phial after the manner described, hung on a tripod for a philosophical month, and warmed with a very gentle fire; although, if the fire be regulated in dire proportion this operation is concluded in thirty-one days, and brought to perfection. By this, Mercury and any other imperfect metals acquire the perfection of gold.

CHAPTER XV.

CONCERNING THE PROJECTION TO BE MADE BY THE MYSTERY AND ARCANUM OF ANTIMONY.

No precise weight can be assigned in this work of projection, though the tincture itself may be extracted from a certain subject, in a defined proportion, and with fitting appliances. For instance, that Medicine tinges sometimes thirty, forty, occasionally even sixty, eighty, or a hundred parts of the imperfect metal. So, then, the whole business hinges chiefly on the purification of the Medicine and the industry of the operator, and, next, on the greater; or lesser cleanliness and purity of the imperfect body taken in hand. For instance, one Venus is more pure than another; and hence it happens that no one fixed weight can be specified in projection. This alone is worth noting, that if the operator happens to have taken too much of the tincture, he can correct this mistake by adding more of the imperfect metal. But if there be too much of the subject, so that the powers of the tincture are weakened, this error is easily remedied by a cineritium, or by cementations, or by ablutions in crude Antimony. There is nothing at this stage which need delay the operator; only let him put before himself a fact which has been passed over by the philosophers, and by some studiously veiled, namely, that in projections there must be a revivification, that is to say, an animation of imperfect bodies – nay, so to speak, a spiritualisation; concerning which some have said that their metals are no common ones, since they live and have a soul.

ANIMATION IS PRODUCED IN THE FOLLOWING WAY.

Take of Venus, wrought into small plates, as much as you will, ten, twenty, or forty pounds. Let these be incrusted with a pulse made of arsenic and calcined tartar, and calcined in their own vessel for twenty-four hours. Then at length let the Venus be pulverised, washed, and thoroughly purified. Let the calcination with ablution be repeated three or four times. In this way it is purged and purified from its thick greenness and from its own impure sulphur. You will have to be on your guard against calcinations made with common sulphur. For whatever is good in the metal is spoilt thereby, and what is bad becomes worse. To ten marks of this purged Venus add one of pure Luna. But in order that the work of the Medicine may be accelerated by projection, and may more easily penetrate the imperfect body, and drive out all portions which are opposed to the nature of Luna, this is accomplished by means of a perfect ferment. For the work is defiled by means of an impure Sulphur, so that a cloud is stretched out over the surface of the transmuted substance, or the metal is mixed with the loppings of the Sulphur and may be cast away therewith. But if a projection of a red stone is to be made, with a view to a red transmutation, it must first fall on gold, afterwards on silver, or on some other metal thoroughly purified, as we have directed above. From thence arises the most perfect gold.

CHAPTER XVI.

CONCERNING THE UNIVERSAL MATTER OF THE PHILOSOPHERS' STONE.

After the mortification of vegetables, they are transmuted, by the concurrence of two minerals, such as Sulphur and Salt, into a mineral nature, so that at length they themselves become perfect minerals. So it is that in the mineral burrows and caves of the earth, vegetables are found which, in the long succession of time, and by the continuous heat of sulphur, put off the vegetable nature and assume that of the mineral. This happens, for the most part, where the appropriate nutriment is taken away from vegetables of this kind, so that they are afterwards compelled to derive their nourishment from the sulphur and salts of the earth, until what was before vegetable passes over into a perfect mineral. From this mineral state, too, sometimes a perfect metallic essence arises, and this happens by the progress of one degree into another.

But let us return to the Philosophers' Stone. The matter of this, as certain writers have mentioned, is above all else difficult to discover and abstruse to understand. The method and most certain rule for finding out this, as well as other subjects – what they embrace or are able to effect – is a careful examination of the root and seed by which they come to our knowledge. For this, before all things else, a consideration of principles is absolutely necessary; and also of the manner in which Nature proceeds from imperfection to the end of perfection. Now, for this consideration it is well to have it thoroughly understood from the first that all things created by Nature consist of three primal elements, namely, natural Mercury, Sulphur, and Salt in combination, so that in some substances they are volatile, in others fixed. Wherever corporal Salt is mixed with spiritual Mercury and animated Sulphur into one body, then Nature begins to work, in those subterranean places which serve for her vessels, by means of a separating fire. By this the thick and impure Sulphur is separated from the pure, the earth is segregated from the Salt, and the clouds from the Mercury, while those purer parts are preserved, which Nature again welds together into a pure geogamic body. This operation is esteemed by the Magi as a mixture and conjunction by the uniting of three constituents, body, soul, and spirit. When this union is completed there results from it a pure Mercury. Now if this, when flowing down through its subterranean passages and veins, meets with a chaotic Sulphur, the Mercury is coagulated by it according to the condition of the Sulphur. It is, however, still volatile, so that scarcely in a hundred years is it transformed into a metal. Hence arose the vulgar idea that Mercury and Sulphur are the matter of the metals, as is certainly reported by miners. It is not, however, common Mercury and common Sulphur which are the matter of the metals, but the Mercury and the Sulphur of the philosophers are incorporated and inborn in perfect metals, and in the forms of them, so that they never fly from the fire, nor are they depraved by the force of the corruption caused by the elements. It is true that by the dissolution of this natural mixture our Mercury is subdued, as all the philosophers say. Under this form of words our Mercury comes to be drawn from perfect bodies and from the forces of the earthly planets. This is what Hermes asserts in the following terms: "The Sun and the Moon are the roots of this Art". The Son of Hamuel says that the Stone of the philosophers is water coagulated, namely, in Sol and Luna. From this it is clearer than the sun that the material of the Stone is nothing else but Sol and Luna. This is confirmed by the fact that like produces like. We know that there are only two Stones, the white and the red. There are also two matters of the Stone, Sol and Luna, formed together in a proper marriage, both natural and artificial. Now, as we see that the man or the woman, without the seed of both, cannot generate, in the same way our man, Sol, and his wife, Luna, cannot conceive or do an thing in the way of generation, without the seed and sperm of both. Hence the philosophers gathered that a third thing was necessary, namely, the animated seed of both, the man and the woman, without which they judged that the whole of their work was fruitless and in vain. Such a sperm is Mercury, which, by the natural conjunction of both bodies Sol and Luna, receives their nature into itself in union. Then at length, and not before, the work is fit for congress, ingress, and generation; by the masculine and feminine power and virtue. Hence the philosophers have said that this same Mercury is composed of body, spirit, and soul, and that it has assumed the nature and property of all elements. Therefore, with their most powerful genius and intellect, they asserted their Stone to be animal. They even called it their Adam, who carries his own invisible Eve hidden in his body, from that moment in which they were united by the power of the Supreme God, the Maker of all creatures. For this reason it may be said that the Mercury of the Philosophers is none other than their most abstruse, compounded Mercury, and not the common Mercury. So then they have wisely said to the sages that there is in Mercury whatever wise men seek. Almadir, the philosopher, says: "We extract our Mercury from one perfect body and two perfect natural conditions incorporated together, which indeed puts forth externally its perfection, whereby it is able to resist the fire, so that its internal imperfection may be protected by the external perfections". By this passage of the sagacious philosopher is understood the Adamic matter, the limbus of the microcosm[16], and the homogeneous, unique matter of the philosophers. The sayings of these men, which we have before mentioned, are simply golden, and ever to be held in the highest esteem, because they contain nothing superfluous or without force. Summarily, then, the matter of the Philosophers' Stone is none other than a fiery and perfect Mercury extracted by Nature and Art; that is, the artificially prepared and true hermaphrodite Adam, and the microcosm: That wisest of the philosophers, Mercurius, making the same statement, called the Stone an orphan. Our Mercury, therefore, is the same which contains in itself all the perfections, force, and virtues of the Sun, which also runs through all the streets and houses of all the planets, and in its own rebirth has acquired the force of things above and things below; to the marriage of which it is to be compared, as is clear from the whiteness and the redness combined in it.

CHAPTER XVII.

CONCERNING THE PREPARATION OF THE MATTER FOR THE PHILOSOPHIC STONE.

What Nature principally requires is that its own philosophic man should be brought into a mercurial substance, so that it may be born into the philosophic Stone. Moreover, it should be remarked that those common preparations of Geber, Albertus Magnus, Thomas Aquinas, Rupescissa, Polydorus, and such men, are nothing more than some particular solutions, sublimations, and calcinations, having no reference to our universal substance, which needs only the most secret fire of the philosophers. Let the fire and Azoth therefore suffice for you. From the fact that the philosophers make mention of certain preparations, such as putrefaction, distillation, sublimation, calcination, coagulation, dealbation, rubification, ceration, fixation, and the like, you should understand that in their universal substance, Nature herself fulfils all the operations in the matter spoken of, and not the operator, only in a philosophical vessel, and with a similar fire, but not common fire. The white and the red spring from one root without any intermediary. It is dissolved by itself, it copulates by itself, grows white, grows red, is made crocus-coloured and black by itself, marries itself and conceives in itself. It is therefore to be decocted, to be baked, to be fused; it ascends, and it descends. All these operations are a single operation and produced by the fire alone. Still, some philosophers, nevertheless, have, by a highly graduated essence of wine, dissolved the body of Sol, and rendered it volatile, so that it should ascend through an alembic, thinking that this is the true volatile matter of the philosophers, though it is not so. And although it be no contemptible arcanum to reduce this perfect metallic body into a volatile, spiritual substance, yet they are wrong in their separation of the elements. This process of the monks, such as Lully, Richard of England, Rupescissa, and the rest, is erroneous. By this process they thought that they were going to separate gold after this fashion into a subtle, spiritual, and elementary power, each by itself, and afterwards by circulation and rectification to combine them again in one – but in vain. For although one element may, in a certain sense, be separated from another, yet, nevertheless, every element separated in this way can again be separated into another element, but these elements cannot afterwards by circulation in a pelican, or by distillation, be again brought back into one; but they always remain a certain volatile matter, and aurum potabile, as they themselves call it. The reason why they could not compass their intention is that Nature refuses to be in this way dragged asunder and separated by man's disjunctions, as by earthly glasses and instruments. She alone knows her own operations and the weights of the elements, the separations, rectifications, and copulations of which she brings about without the aid of any operator or manual artifice, provided only the matter be contained in the secret fire and in its proper occult vessel. The separation of the elements, therefore, is impossible by man. It may appear to take place, but it is not true, whatever may be said by Raymond Lully, and of that famous English golden work which he is falsely supposed to have accomplished. Nature herself has within herself the proper separator, who again joins together what he has put asunder, without the aid of man. She knows best the proportion of every element, which man does not know, however miseading writers romance in their frivolous and false recipes about this volatile gold.

This is the opinion of the philosophers, that when they have put their matter into the more secret fire, and when with a moderated philosophical heat it is cherished on every side, beginning to pass into corruption, it grows black. This operation they term putrefaction, and they call the blackness by the name of the Crow's Head. The ascent and descent thereof they term distillation, ascension, and descension. The exsiccation they call coagulation; and the dealbation they call calcination; while because it becomes fluid and soft in the heat they make mention of ceration. When it ceases to ascend and remains liquid at the bottom, they say fixation is present.

In this manner it is the terms of philosophical operations are to be understood, and not otherwise.

CHAPTER XVIII.

CONCERNING INSTRUMENTS AND THE PHILOSOPHIC VESSEL.

Sham philosophers have misunderstood the occult and secret philosophic vessel, and worse is that which is said by Aristoteles the Alchemist (not the famous Greek Academic Philosopher), giving it out that the matter is to be decocted in a triple vessel. Worst of all is that which is said by another, namely, that the matter in its first separation and first degree requires a metallic vessel; in its second degree of coagulation and dealbation of its earth a glass vessel; and in the third degree, for fixation, an earthen vessel. Nevertheless, hereby the philosophers understand one vessel alone in all the operations up to the perfection of the red stone. Since, then, our matter is our root for the white and the red, necessarily our vessel must be so fashioned that the matter in it may be governed by the heavenly bodies. For invisible celestial influences and the impressions of the stars are in the very first degree necessary for the work: Otherwise it would be impossible for the Oriental, Chaldean, and Egyptian stone to be realised. By this Anaxagoras knew the powers of the whole firmament, and foretold that a great stone would descend from heaven to earth, which actually happened after his death. To the Cabalists our vessel is perfectly well known, because it must be made according to a truly geometrical proportion and measure, and from a definite quadrature of the circle, so that the spirit and the soul of our matter, separated from their body, may be able to raise this vessel with themselves in proportion to the altitude of heaven. If the vessel be wider, narrower, higher, or lower than is fitting, and than the dominating operating spirit and soul desire, the heat of our secret philosophic fire (which is, indeed, very severe), will violently excite the matter and urge it on to excessive operation, so that the vessel is shivered into a thousand pieces, with imminent danger to the body and even the life of the operator. On the other hand, if it be of greater capacity than is required in due proportion for the heat to have effect on the matter, the work will be wasted and thrown away. So, then, our philosophic vessel must be made with the greatest care. What the material of the vessel should be is understood only by those who, in the first solution of our fixed and perfected matter have brought that matter to its own primal quintessence. Enough has been said on this point.

The operator must also very accurately note what, in its first solution, the matter sends forth and rejects from itself.

The method of describing the form of the vessel is difficult. It should be such as Nature requires, and it must be sought out and investigated from every possible source, so that, from the height of the philosophic heaven, elevated above the philosophic earth, it may be able to operate on the fruit of its own earthly body. It should have this form, too, in order that the separation and purification of the elements, when the fire drives one from the other, may be able to be accomplished, and that each may have power to occupy the place to which it adheres; and also that the sun and the other planets may exercise their operations around the elemental earth, while their course in their circuit is neither hindered nor agitated with too swift a motion. In all these particulars which have been mentioned it must have a proper proportion of rotundity and of height.

The instruments for the first purification of mineral bodies are fusing-vessels, bellows, tongs, capels, cupels, tests, cementatory vessels, cineritiums, cucurbites, bocias for aquafortis and aqua regia; and also the appliances which are required for projection at the climax of the work.

CHAPTER XIX.

CONCERNING THE SECRET FIRE OF THE PHILOSOPHERS.

This is a well-known sententious saying of the philosophers, "Let fire and Azoc suffice thee". Fire alone is the whole work and the entire art. Moreover, they who build their fire and keep their vessel in that heat are in error. In vain some have attempted it with the heat of horse dung. By the coal fire, without a medium, they have sublimated their matter, but they have not dissolved it. Others have got their heat from lamps, asserting that this is the secret fire of the philosophers for making their Stone. Some have placed it in a bath, first of all in heaps of ants' eggs; others in juniper ashes. Some have sought the fire in quicklime, in tartar, vitriol, nitre, etc. Others, again, have sought it in boiling water. Thomas Aquinas speaks falsely of this fire, saying that God and the angels cannot do without this fire, but use it daily. What blasphemy is this! Is it not a manifest lie that God is not able to do without the elemental heat of boiling water? All the heats excited by those means which have been mentioned are utterly useless for our work Take care not to be misled by Arnold de Villa Nova, who has written on the subject of the coal fire, for in this matter he will deceive you.

Almadir says that the invisible rays of our fire of themselves suffice. Another cites, as an illustration, that the heavenly heat by its reflections tends to the coagulation and perfection of Mercury, just as by its continual motion it tends to the generation of metals. Again, says this same authority, "Make a fire, vaporous, digesting, as for cooking, continuous, but not volatile or boiling, enclosed, shut off from the air, not burning, but altering and penetrating. Now, in truth, I have mentioned every mode of fire and of exciting heat. If you are a true philosopher you will understand". This is what he says.

Salmanazar remarks: "Ours is a corrosive fire, which brings over our vessel an air like a cloud, in which cloud the rays of this fire are hidden. If this dew of chaos and this moisture of the cloud fail, a mistake has been committed". Again, Almadir says, that unless the fire has warmed our sun with its moisture, by the excrement of the mountain, with a moderate ascent, we shall not be partakers either of the Red or the White Stone.

All these matters shew quite openly to us the occult fire of the wise men. Finally, this is the matter of our fire, namely, that it be kindled by the quiet spirit of sensible fire, which drives upwards, as it were, the heated chaos from the opposite quarter, and above our philosophic matter. This heat, glowing above our vessel, must urge it to the motion of a perfect generation, temperately but continuously, without intermission.

CHAPTER XX.

CONCERNING THE FERMENT OF THE PHILOSOPHERS, AND THE WEIGHT.

Philosophers have laboured greatly in the art of ferments and of fermentations, which seems important above all others. With reference thereto some have made a vow to God and to the philosophers that they would never divulge its arcanum by similitudes or by parables.

Nevertheless, Hermes, the father of all philosophers, in the "Book of the Seven Treatises", most clearly discloses the secret of ferments, saying that they consist only of their own paste; and more at length he says that the ferment whitens the confection, hinders combustion, altogether retards the flux of the tincture, consoles bodies, and amplifies unions. He says, also, that this is the key and the end of the work, concluding that the ferment is nothing but paste, as that of the sun is nothing but sun, and that of the moon nothing but moon. Others affirm that the ferment is the soul, and if this be not rightly prepared from the magistery, it effects nothing. Some zealots of this Art seek the Art in common sulphur, arsenic, tutia, auripigment, vitriol, etc., but in vain; since the substance which is sought is the same as that from which it has to be drawn forth. It should be remarked, therefore, that fermentations of this kind do not succeed according to the wishes of the zealots in the way they desire, but, as is clear from what has been said above, simply in the way of natural successes.

But, to come at length to the weight; this must be noted in two ways. The first is natural, the second artificial. The natural attains its result in the earth by Nature and concordance. Of this, Arnold says: If more or less earth than Nature requires be added, the soul is suffocated, and no result is perceived, nor any fixation. It is the same with the water. If more or less of this be taken it will bring a corresponding loss. A superfluity renders the matter unduly moist, and a deficiency makes it too dry and too hard. If there be over much air present, it is too strongly impressed on the tincture; if there be too little, the body will turn out pallid. In the same way, if the fire be too strong, the matter is burnt up; if it be too slack, it has not the power of drying, nor of dissolving or heating the other elements. In these things elemental heat consists.

Artificial weight is quite occult. It is comprised in the magical art of ponderations. Between the spirit, soul, and body, say the philosophers, weight consists of Sulphur as the director of the work; for the soul strongly desires Sulphur, and necessarily observes it by reason of its weight.

You can understand it thus: Our matter is united to a red fixed Sulphur, to which a third part of the regimen has been entrusted, even to the ultimate degree, so that it may perfect to infinity the operation of the Stone, may remain therewith together with its fire, and may consist of a weight equal to the matter itself, in and through all, without variation of any degree. Therefore, after the matter has been adapted and mixed in its proportionate weight, it should be closely shut up with its seal in the vessel of the philosophers, and committed to the secret fire. In this the Philosophic Sun will rise and surge up, and will illuminate all things that have been looking for his light, expecting it with highest hope.

In these few words we will conclude the arcanum of the Stone, an arcanum which is in no way maimed or defective, for which we give God undying thanks. Now have we opened to you our treasure, which is not to be paid for by the riches of the whole world.

HERE ENDS THE AURORA OF THE PHILOSOPHERS.

NOTES

[1] The work under this title is cited occasionally in other writings of Paracelsus, but is not included in the great folio published at Geneva in 1688. It was first issued at Basle in 1575, and was accompanied with copious annotations in Latin by the editor, Gerard Dorne. This personage was a very persevering collector of the literary remains of Paracelsus, but is not altogether free from the suspicion of having elaborated his original. The Aurora is by some regarded as an instance in point; though no doubt in the main it is a genuine work of the Sage of Hohenheim, yet in some respects it does seem to approximate somewhat closely to previous schools of Alchemy, which can scarcely he regarded as representing the actual standpoint of Paracelsus.

[2] He who created man the same also created science. What has man in any place without labour? When the mandate went forth: Thou shalt live by the sweat of thy brow, there was, as it were, a new creation. When God uttered His fiat the world was made. Art, however, was not then made, nor was the light of Nature. But when Adam was expelled from Paradise, God created for him the light of Nature when He bade him live by the work of his hands. In like manner, He created for Eve her special light when He said to her: In sorrow shalt thou bring forth children. Thus, and there, were these beings made human and earthy that were before like angelicals. ... Thus, by the word were creatures made, and by this same word was also made the light which was necessary to man. ... Hence the interior man followed from the second creation, after the expulsion from Paradise. ... Before the Fall, that cognition which was requisite to man had not begun to develop in him. He received it from the angel when he was cast out of Paradise. ... Man was made complete in the order of the body, but not in the order of the arts. – *De Caducis*, Par. III.

[3] No work precisely corresponding co this title is extant among the writings of Paracelsus. The subjects to which reference is made are discussed in the *Philosophia Sagax*.

[4] Before all things it is necessary to have a right understanding of the nature of Celestial Magic. It originates from divine virtue. There is that magic which Moses practised, and there is the maleficent magic of the sorcerers. There are, then, different kinds of Magi. So also there is what is called the Magic of Nature; there is the Celestial Magus; there is the Magus of Faith, that is, one

whose faith makes him whole. There is, lastly, the Magus of Perdition. – *Philosophia Sagax*, Lib. II., c. 6.

⁵ Learn, therefore, Astronomic Magic, which otherwise I call cabalistic. – *De Pestilitate*, Tract I. This art, formerly called cabalistic, was in the beginning named caballa, and afterwards caballia. It is a species of magic. It was also, but falsely, called Gabanala, by one whose knowledge of the subject was profound. It was of an unknown Ethnic origin, and it passed subsequently to the Chaldaeans and Hebrews, by both of whom it was corrupted. – *Philosophia Sagax*, Lib. I., s. v. *Probatio in Scientiam Nectromantricam*.

⁶ The object which received the influence and exhibited the sign thereof appears to have been termed Gamaheu, Gamahey etc. But the name was chiefly given to certain stones on which various and wonderful images and figures of men and animals have been found naturally depicted, being no work of man, but the result of the providence and counsel of God. – *De Imaginibus*, c. 7 and c. 13. It is possible, magically, for a man to project his infiuence into these stones and some other substances. – *Ibid.*, c. 13. But they also have their own inherent virtue, which is indicated by the shape and the special nature of the impression. – *Ibid.*, c. 7. There was also an artificial Gamaheus invented and prepared by the Magi, and this seems to have been more powerful. – *De Carduo Angelico*.

⁷ Man was regarded by Paracelsus as himself in a special manner the true Quintessence. After God had created all the elements, stars, and every other created thing, and had disposed them according to His will, He proceeded, lastly, to the forming of man. He extracted the essence out of the four elements into one mass; He extracted also the essence of wisdom, art, and reason out of the stars, and this twofold essence He congested into one mass: which mass Scripture calls the slime of the earth. From that mass two bodies were made – the sidereal and the elementary. These, according to the light of Nature, are called the *quintum esse*. The mass was extracted, and therein the firmament and the elements were condensed. What was extracted from the four after this manner constituted a fifth. The Quintessence is the nucleus and the place of the essences and properties of all things in the universal world. All nature came into the hand of God – all potency, all property, all essence of the superior and inferior globe. All these had God joined in His hand, and from these He formed man according to His image. – *Philosophia Sagax*, Lib. I., c. 2.

⁸ All created things proceed from the coagulated, and after coagulation must go on to resolution. From resolution proceed all procreated things. – *De Tartaro* (fragment). All bodies of minerals are coagulated by salt. – *De Natraralibus Aquis*, Lib. III., Tract 2.

⁹ So acute is the potency of calcined blood, that if it be poured slowly on iron it produces in the first place a whiteness thereon, and then generates rust. – *Scholia in Libros de Tartaro*. In Lib. II., Tract II.

¹⁰ One recipe for the fixation of arsenic is as follows: – Take equal parts of arsenic and nitre. Place these in a tigillum, set upon coals so that they may begin to boil and to evaporate. Continue till ebullition and evaporation cease, and the substances shall have settled to the bottom of the vessel like fat melting in a frying-pan; then, for the space of an hour and a half (the longer the better), set it apart to settle. Subsequently pour the compound upon marble, and it will acquire a gold colour. In a damp place it will assume the consistency of a fatty fluid. – *De Naturalibus Rebus*, c. 9. Again: The fixation of arsenic is performed by salt of urine, after which it is converted by itself into an oil. – *Chirurgia Minor*, Lib. II.

¹¹ Concerning the kinds of arsenic, it is to be noted that there are those which flow forth from their proper mineral or metal, and are called native arsenics. Next there are arsenics out of metals after their kind. Then there are those made by Art through transmutation. White or crystalline arsenic is the best for medicine Yellow and red arsenic are utilised by chemists for investigating the transmutation of metals, in which arsenic has a special efficacy. – *De Naturalibus Rebus*, c. 9.

¹² The arcanum of vitriol is the oil of vitriol. Thus: after the aquosity has been removed in coction from vitriol, the spirit is elicited by the application of greater heat. The vitriol then comes over pure in the form of water. This water is combined with the *caput mortuum* left by the process, and on again separating in a *balneum maris*, the phlegmatic part passes off, and the oil, or the arcanum of vitriol, remains at the bottom of the vessel. – *Ibid*.

¹³ So long as the viridity or greenness of vitriol subsists therein, it is of a soft quality and substance. But if it be excocted so that it is deprived of its moisture, it is thereby changed into a hard stone from which even fire can be struck. When the moisture is evaporated from vitriol, the sulphur which it contains

predominates over the salt, and the vitriol turns red. – *De Pestilitate*, Tract I.

[14] The diagnosis of vitriol is concerned with it both in Medicine and Alchemy. In Medicine it is a paramount remedy. In Alchemy it has many additional purposes. The Art of Medicine and Alchemy consists in the preparation of vitriol, for it is worthless in its crude state. It is like unto wood, out of which it is possible to carve anything. Three kinds of oil are extracted from vitriol – a red oil, by distillation in a retort after an alchemistic method, and this is the most acid of all substances, and has also a corrosive quality – also a green and a white oil, distilled from crude vitriol by descension. – *De Vitriolo*. Nor let it be regarded as absurd that we assign such great virtues to vitriol, for therein resides, secret and hidden, a certain peculiar golden force, not corporeal but spiritual, which excellent and admirable virtue exists in greater potency and certainty therein than it does in gold. When this golden spirit of vitriol is volatilized and separated from its impurities, so that the essence alone remains, it is like unto potable gold. – *De Morbis Amentium, Methodus* II., c. 1.

[15] Antimony can be made into a pap with the water of vitriol, and then purified by sal ammoniac, and in this manner there may be obtained from it a thick purple or reddish liquor. This is oil of antimony, and it has many virtues. – *Chirurgia Magna*, Lib. V. Take three pounds of antimony and as much of sal gemmae. Distil them together in a retort for three natural days, and so you will have a red oil, which has incredible healing power in cases of otherwise incurable wounds. – *Chirurgia Minor*, Tract II., c. 11.

[16] Man himself was created from that which is termed limbus. This limbus contained the potency and nature of all creatures. Hence man himself is called the microcosmus, or world in miniature. – *De Generatione Stultorum*. Man was fashioned out of the limbus, and this limbus is the universal world. –*Paramirum Aliud*, Lib. II., c. 2. The limbus was the first matter of man. ... Whosoever knows the limbus knows also what mam is. Whatsoever the limbus is, that also is man. – *Paramirum Aliud*, Lib. IV. There is a dual limbus, man, the lesser limbus, and that Great Limbus from which he was produced. – *De Podagra*, s. v. *de Limbo*. The limbus is the seed out of which all creatures are produced and grow, as the tree comes forth from its own special seed. The limbus has its ground in the word of God. – *Ibid*. The limbus of Adam was haven and earth, water and air. Therefore,

man also remains in the limbus, and contains in himself heaven and earth, air and water, and these things he also himself is. – *Paragranum Alterum*, Tract II.

A SHORT CATECHISM OF ALCHEMY

A SHORT CATECHISM OF ALCHEMY

Q. What is the chief study of a Philosopher?
A. It is the investigation of the operations of Nature.
Q. What is the end of Nature?
A. God, Who is also its beginning.
Q. Whence are all things derived?
A. From one and indivisible Nature.
Q. Into how many regions is Nature separated?
A. Into four palmary regions.
Q. Which are they?
A. The dry, the moist, the warm, and the cold, which are the four elementary qualities, whence all things originate.
Q. How is Nature differentiated?
A. Into male and female.
Q. To what may we compare Nature?
A. To Mercury.
Q. Give a concise definition of Nature.
A. It is not visible, though it operates visibly; for it is simply a volatile spirit, fulfilling its office in bodies, and animated by the universal spirit-the divine breath, the central and universal fire, which vivifies all things that exist.
Q. What should be the qualities possessed by the examiners of Nature?
A. They should be like unto Nature herself. That is to say, they should be truthful, simple, patient, and persevering.
Q. What matters should subsequently engross their attention?
A. The philosophers should most carefully ascertain whether their designs are in harmony with Nature, and of a possible and

attainable kind; if they would accomplish by their own power anything that is usually performed by the power of Nature, they must imitate her in every detail.

Q. What method must be followed in order to produce something which shall be developed to a superior degree than Nature herself develops it.

A. The manner of its improvement must be studied, and this is invariably operated by means of a like nature. For example, if it be desired to develop the intrinsic virtue of a given metal beyond its natural condition, the chemist must avail himself of the metallic nature itself, and must be able to discriminate between its male and female differentiations.

Q. Where does the metallic nature store her seeds?

A. In the four elements.

Q. With what materials can the philosopher alone accomplish anything?

A. With the germ of the given matter; this is its elixir or quintessence, more precious by far, and more useful, to the artist, than is Nature herself. Before the philosopher has extracted the seed, or germ, Nature, in his behalf, will be ready to perform her duty.

Q. What is the germ, or seed, of any substance?

A. It is the most subtle and perfect decoction and digestion of the substance itself; or, rather, it is the Balm of Sulphur, which is identical with the Radical Moisture of Metals.

Q. By what is this seed, or germ, engendered?

A. By the four elements, subject to the will of the Supreme Being, and through the direct intervention of the imagination of Nature.

Q. After what manner do the four elements operate?

A. By means of an incessant and uniform motion, each one, according to its quality, depositing its seed in the centre of the earth, where it is subjected to action and digested, and is subsequently expelled in an outward direction by the laws of movement.

Q. What do the philosophers understand by the centre of the earth?

A. A certain void place where nothing may repose, and the existence of which is assumed.

Q. Where, then, do the four elements expel and deposit their seeds?

A. In the ex-centre, or in the margin and circumference of the centre, which, after it has appropriated a portion, casts out the surplus into the region of excrement, scoriae, fire, and formless chaos.

Q. Illustrate this teaching by an example.

A. Take any level table, and set in its centre a vase filled with water; surround the vase with several things of various colours, especially salt, taking care that a proper distance intervenes between them all. Then pour out the water from the vase, and it will flow in streams here and there; one will encounter a substance of a red colour, and will assume a tinge of red; another will pass over the salt, and will contract a saline flavour; for it is certain that water does not modify the places which it traverses, but the diverse characteristics of places change the nature of water. In the same way the seed which is deposited by the four elements at the centre of the earth is subject to a variety of modifications in the places through which it passes, so that every existing substance is produced in the likeness of its channel, and when a seed on its arrival at a certain point encounters pure earth and pure water, a pure substance results, but the contrary in an opposite case.

Q. After what manner do the elements procreate this seed?

A. In order to the complete elucidation of this point, it must be observed that there are two gross and heavy elements and two that are volatile in character. Two, in like manner, are dry and two humid, one out of the four being actually excessively dry, and the other excessively moist. They are also masculine and feminine. Now, each of them has a marked tendency to reproduce its own species within its own sphere. Moreover, they are never in repose, but are perpetually interacting, and each of them separates, of and by itself, the most subtle portion thereof. Their general place of meeting is in the centre, even the centre of the Archeus, that servant of Nature, where coming to mix their several seeds, they agitate and finally expel them to the exterior.

Q. What is the true and the first matter of all metals?

A. The first matter, properly so called, is dual in its essence, or is in itself of a twofold nature; one, nevertheless, cannot create a metal without the concurrence of the other. The first and the palmary essence is an aerial humidity, blended with a warm air, in the form of a fatty water, which adheres to all substances indiscriminately, whether they are pure or impure.

Q. How has this humidity been named by Philosophers?
A. Mercury.
Q. By what is it governed?
A. By the rays of the Sun and Moon.
Q. What is the second matter?
A. The warmth of the earth -otherwise, that dry heat which is termed Sulphur by the Philosophers.
Q. Can the entire material body be converted into seed?
A. Its eight-hundredth part only-that, namely, which is secreted in the centre of the body in question, and may, for example, be seen in a grain of wheat.
Q. Of what use is the bulk of the matter as regards its seed?
A. It is useful as a safeguard against excessive heat, cold, moisture, or aridity, and, in general, all hurtful inclemency, against which it acts as an envelope.
Q. Would those artists who pretend to reduce the whole matter of any body into seed derive any advantage from the process, supposing it were possible to perform it?
A. None; on the contrary, their labour would be wholly unproductive, because nothing that is good can be accomplished by a deviation from natural methods.
Q. What, therefore, should be done?
A. The matter must be effectively separated from its impurities, for there is no metal, how pure soever, which is entirely free from imperfections, though their extent varies. Now all superfluities, cortices, and scoriae must be peeled off and purged out from the matter in order to discover its seed.
Q. What should receive the most careful attention of the Philosopher?
A. Assuredly, the end of Nature, and this is by no means to be looked for in the vulgar metals, because, these having issued already from the hands of the fashioner, it is no longer to be found therein.
Q. For what precise reason?
A. Because the vulgar metals, and chiefly gold, are absolutely dead, while ours, on the contrary, are absolutely living, and possess a soul.
Q. What is the life of metals?
A. It is no other substance than fire, when they are as yet imbedded in the mines.

Q. What is their death?
A. Their life and death are in reality one principle, for they die, as they live, by fire, but their death is from a fire of fusion.
Q. After what manner are metals conceived in the womb of the earth?
A. When the four elements have developed their power or virtue in the centre of the earth, and have deposited their seed, the Archeus of Nature, in the course of a distillatory process, sublimes them superficially by the warmth and energy of the perpetual movement.
Q. Into what does the wind resolve itself when it is distilled through the pores of the earth?
A. It resolves itself into water, whence all things spring; in this state it is merely a humid vapour, out of which there is subsequently evolved the principiated principle of all substances, which also serves as the first matter of the Philosophers.
Q. What then is this principiated principle, which is made use of as the first matter by the Children of Knowledge in the philosophic achievement?
A. It is this identical matter, which, the moment it is conceived, receives a permanent and unchangeable form.
Q. Are Saturn, Jupiter, Mars, Venus, the Sun, the Moon, etc., separately endowed with individual seed?
A. One is common to them all; their differences are to be accounted for by the: locality from which they are derived, not to speak of the fact that Nature completes her work with far greater rapidity in the procreation of silver than in that of gold, and so of the other metals, each in its own proportion.
Q. How is gold formed in the bowels of the earth?
A. When this vapour, of which we have spoken, is sublimed in the centre of the earth, and when it has passed through warm and pure places, where a certain sulphureous grease adheres to the channels, then this vapour, which the Philosophers have denominated their Mercury, becomes adapted and joined to this grease, which it sublimes with itself; from such amalgamation there is produced a certain unctuousness, which, abandoning the vaporous form, assumes that of grease, and is sublimised in other places, which have been cleansed by this preceding vapour, and the earth whereof has consequently been rendered more subtle, pure, and humid; it fills the pores of this earth, is joined thereto, and gold is produced as a result.

Q. How is Saturn engendered?
A. It occurs when the said unctuosity, or grease, passes through places which are totally impure and cold.
Q. How is Venus brought forth?
A. She is produced in localities where the earth itself is pure, but is mingled with impure sulphur.
Q. What power does the vapour, which we have recently mentioned, possess in the centre of the earth?
A. By its continual progress it has the power of perpetually rarefying whatsoever is crude and impure, and of successively attracting to itself all that is pure around it.
Q. What is the seed of the first matter of all things?
A. The first matter of things, that is to say, the matter of principiating principles is begotten by Nature, without the assistance of any other seed; in other words, Nature receives the matter from the elements, whence it subsequently brings forth the seed.
Q. What, absolutely speaking, is therefore the seed of things?
A. The seed in a body is no other thing than a congealed air, or a humid vapour, which is useless except it be dissolved by a warm vapour.
Q. How is the generation of seed comprised in the metallic kingdom?
A. By the artifice of Archeus the four elements, in the first generation of Nature, distil a ponderous vapour of water into the centre of the earth ; this is the seed of metals, and it is called Mercury, not on account of its essence, but because of its fluidity, and the facility with which it will adhere to each and every thing.
Q. Why is this vapour compared to sulphur?
A. Because of its internal heat.
Q. From what species of Mercury are we to conclude that the metals are composed?
A. The reference is exclusively to the Mercury of the Philosophers, and in no sense to the common or vulgar substance, which cannot become a seed, seeing that, like other metals, it already contains its own seed.
Q. What, therefore, must actually be accepted as the subject of our matter?
A. The seed alone, otherwise the fixed grain, and not the whole body, which is differentiated into Sulphur, or living male, and into Mercury, or living female.

Q. What operation must be afterwards performed
A. They must be joined together, so that they may form a germ, after which they will proceed to the procreation of a fruit which is conformed to their nature.
Q. What is the part of the artist in this operation?
A. The artist must do nothing but separate that which is subtle from that which is gross.
Q. To what, therefore, is the whole philosophic combination reduced?
A. The development of one into two, and the reduction of two into one, and nothing further.
Q. Whither must we turn for the seed and life of meals and minerals?
A. The seed of minerals is properly the water which exists in the centre
And the heart of the minerals.
Q. How does Nature operate by the help of Art?
A. Every seed, whatsoever its kind, is useless, unless by Nature or Art it is placed in a suitable matrix, where it receives its life by the coction of the germ! and by the congelation of the pure particle, or fixed grain.
Q. How is the seed subsequently nourished and preserved?
A. By the warmth of its body.
Q. What is therefore performed by the artist in the mineral kingdom?
A. He finishes what cannot be finished by Nature on account of the crudity of the air, which has permeated the pores of all bodies by its violence, but on the surface and not in the bowels of the earth.
Q. What correspondence have the metals among themselves?
A. It is necessary for a proper comprehension of the nature of this correspondence to consider the position of the planets, and to pay attention to Saturn, which is the highest of all, and then is succeeded by Jupiter, next by Mars, the Sun, Venus, Mercury, and, lastly, by the Moon. It must be observed that the influential virtues of the planets do not ascend but descend, and experience teaches us that Mars can be easily converted into Venus, not Venus into Mars, which is of a lower sphere. So, also, Jupiter can be easily transmuted into Mercury, because Jupiter is superior to Mercury, the one being second after the firmament, the other second above the earth, and Saturn is highest of all, while the

Moon is lowest. The Sun enters into all, but it is never ameliorated by its inferiors. It is clear that there is a large correspondence between Saturn and the Moon, in the middle of which is the Sun; but to all these changes the Philosopher should strive to administer the Sun.

Q. When the Philosophers speak of gold and silver, from which they extract their matter, are we to suppose that they refer to the vulgar gold and silver?

A. By no means; vulgar silver and gold are dead, while those of the Philosophers are full of life.

Q. What is the object of research among the Philosophers?

A. Proficiency in the art of perfecting what Nature has left imperfect in the mineral kingdom, and the attainment of the treasure of the Philosophical Stone.

Q. What is this Stone?

A. The Stone is nothing else than the radical humidity of the elements, perfectly purified and educed into a sovereign fixation, which causes it to perform such great things for health, life being resident exclusively in the humid radical.

Q. In what does the secret of accomplishing this admirable work consist?

A. It consists in knowing how to educe from potentiality into activity the innate warmth, or the fire of Nature, which is enclosed in the centre of the radical humidity.

Q. What are the precautions which must be made use of to guard against failure in the work?

A. Great pains must be taken to eliminate excrements from the matter, and to conserve nothing but the kernel, which contains all the virtue of the compound.

Q. Why does this medicine heal every species of disease?

A. It is not on account of tile variety of its qualities, but simply because it powerfully fortifies the natural warmth, which it gently stimulates, while other physics irritate it by too violent an action.

Q How can you demonstrate to me the truth of the art in the matter of the tincture?

A. Firstly, its truth is founded on the fact that the physical powder, being composed of the same substance as the metals, namely, quicksilver, has the faculty of combining with these in fusion, one nature easily embracing another which is like itself. Secondly, seeing that the imperfection of the base metals is owing to the crudeness of their quicksilver, and to that alone, the physical powder, which is a ripe and decocted quicksilver, and, in itself a pure fire, can easily communicate to them its own maturity, and can transmute them into its nature, after it has attracted their crude humidity, that is to say, their quicksilver, which is the sole substance that transmutes them, the rest being nothing but scoriae and excrements, which are rejected in projection.

Q. What road should the Philosopher follow that he may attain to the knowledge and execution of the physical work?

A. That precisely which was followed by the Great Architect of the Universe in the creation of the world, by observing how the chaos was evolved.

Q. What was the matter of the chaos?

A. It could be nothing else than a humid vapour, because water alone enters into all created substances, which all finish in a strange term, this term being a proper subject for the impression of all forms.

Q. Give me an example to illustrate what you have just stated.

A. An example may be found in the special productions of composite substances, the seeds of which invariably begin by resolving themselves into a certain humour, which is the chaos of the particular matter, whence issues, by a kind of irradiation, the complete form of the plant. Moreover, it should be observed that Holy Scripture makes no mention of anything except water as the material subject whereupon the Spirit of God brooded, nor of anything except light as the universal form of things.

Q. What profit may the Philosopher derive from these considerations, and what should he especially remark in the method of creation which was pursued by the Supreme Being?

A. In the first place he should observe the matter out of which the world was made; he will see that out of this confused mass, the Sovereign Artist began by extracting light, that this light in the same moment dissolved the darkness which covered the face of the earth, and that it served as the universal form of the matter. He will then easily perceive that in the generation of all composite substances, a species of irradiation takes place, and a separation of light and darkness, wherein Nature is an undeviating copyist of her Creator. The Philosopher will equally understand after what manner, by the action of this light, the empyrean, or firmament which divides the superior and inferior waters, was subsequently produced; how the sky was studded with luminous bodies; and how the necessity for the moon arose, which was owing to the space intervening between the things above and the things below; for the moon is an intermediate torch between the superior and the inferior worlds, receiving the celestial influences and communicating them to the earth. Finally he will understand how the Creator, in the gathering of the waters, produced dry land.

Q. How many heavens can you enumerate?

A. Properly there is one only, which is the firmament that divides the waters from the waters. Nevertheless, three are admitted, of which the first is the space that is above the clouds. In this heaven the waters are rarefied, and fall upon the fixed stars, and it is also in this space that the planets and wandering stars perform their revolutions. The second heaven is the firmament of the fixed stars, while the third is the abode of the supercelestial waters.

Q. Why is the rarefaction of the waters confined to the first heaven?

A. Because it is in the nature of rarefied substances to ascend, and because God, in His eternal laws, has assigned its proper sphere to everything.

Q. Why does each celestial body invariably revolve about an axis?

A. It is by reason of the primeval impetus which it received, and by virtue of the same law which will cause any heavy substance suspended from a thread to turn with the same velocity, if the power which impels its motion be always equal.

Q. Why do the superior waters never descend?

A. Because of their extreme rarefaction. It is for this reason that a skilled chemist can derive more profit from the study of rarefaction than from any other science whatsoever.

Q. What is the matter of the firmament?

A. It is properly air, which is more suitable than water as a medium of light.

Q. After the separation of the waters from the dry earth, what was performed by the Creator to originate generation?

A. He created a certain light which was destined for this office; He placed it in the central fire, and moderated this fire by the humidity of water and by the coldness of earth, so as to keep a check upon its energy and adapt it to His design.

Q. What is the action of this central fire?

A. It continually operates upon the nearest humid matter, which it exalts into vapour; now this vapour is the mercury of Nature and the first matter of the three kingdoms.

Q. How is the sulphur of Nature subsequently formed?
A. By the interaction of the central fire and the mercurial vapour.
Q. How is the salt of the sea produced?
A. By the action of the same fire upon aqueous humidity, when the aerial humidity, which is contained therein, has been exhaled.
Q. What should be done by a truly wise Philosopher when he has once mastered the foundation and the order in the procedure of the Great Architect of the Universe in the construction of all that exists in Nature?
A. He should, as far as may be possible, become a faithful copyist of his Creator. In the physical chaos he should make his chaos such as the original actually was; he should separate the light from the darkness : he should form his firmament for the separation of the waters which are above from the waters which are below, and should successively accomplish, point by point, the entire sequence of the creative act.
Q. With what is this grand and sublime operation performed?
A. With one single corpuscle, or minute body, which, so to speak, contains nothing but faeces, filth, and abominations, but whence a certain tenebrous and mercurial humidity is extracted, which contains in itself all that is required by the Philosopher, because, as a fact, he is in search of nothing hut the true Mercury.
Q. What kind of mercury, therefore, must he make use of in performing the work? A. Of a mercury which, as such, is not found on the earth, but is extracted from bodies, yet not from vulgar mercury, as it has been falsely said.
Q. Why is the latter unfitted to the needs of our work?
A. Because the wise artist must take notice that vulgar mercury has an insufficient quantity of sulphur, and he should consequently operate upon a body created by Nature, in which Nature herself has united the sulphur and mercury that it is the work of the artist to separate.
Q. What must he subsequently do?
A. He must purify them and join them anew together.
Q. How do you denominate the body of which we have been speaking?
A. The RUDE STONE, Or Chaos, or Iliaste, or Hyle--that confused mass which is known but universally despised.
Q. As you have told me that Mercury is the one thing which the Philosopher must absolutely understand, will you give me a circumstantial description of it, so as to avoid misconception?

A. In respect of its nature, our Mercury is dual--fixed and volatile; in regard to its motion, it is also dual, for it has a motion of ascent and of descent; by that of descent, it is the influence of plants, by which it stimulates the drooping fire of Nature, and this is its first office previous to congelation. By its ascensional movement, it rises, seeking to be purified, and as this is after congelation, it is considered to be the radical moisture of substances, which, beneath its vile scoriae, still preserves the nobility of its first origin.

Q. How many species of moisture do you suppose to be in each composite thing?

A. There are three--the Elementary, which is properly the vase of the other elements; the Radical, which, accurately speaking, is the oil, or balm, in which the entire virtue of the subject is resident--lastly, the Alimentary, the true natural dissolvent, which draws up the drooping internal fire, causing corruption and blackness by its humidity, and fostering and sustaining the subject.

Q. How many species of Mercury are there known to the Philosophers?

A. The Mercury of the Philosophers may be regarded under four aspects; the first is entitled the Mercury of bodies, which is actually their concealed seed; the second is the Mercury of Nature, which is the Bath or Vase of the Philosophers, otherwise the humid radical; to the third has been applied the designation, Mercury of the Philosophers, because it is found in their laboratory and in their minera. It is the sphere of Saturn; it is the Diana of the Wise; it is the true salt of metals, after the acquisition of which the true philosophic work may be truly said to have begun. In its fourth aspect, it is called Common Mercury, which yet is not that of the Vulgar, but rather is properly the true air of the Philosophers, the true middle substance of water, the true secret and concealed fire, called also common fire, because it is common to all minerae, for it is the substance of metals, and thence do they derive their quantity and quality.

Q. How many operations art comprised in our work?

A. There is one only, which may be resolved into sublimation, and sublimation, according to Geber, is nothing other than the elevation of the dry matter by the mediation of fire, with adherence to its own vase.

Q. What precaution should be taken in reading the Hermetic Philosophers ?

A. Great care, above all, must be observed upon this point, lest what they say upon the subject should be interpreted literally and in accordance with the mere sound of the words: For the letter killeth, but the spirit giveth life.

Q. What books should be read in order to have an acquaintance with our science?

A. Among the ancients, all the works of Hermes should especially be studied; in the next place, a certain book, entitled The Passage of the Red Sea, and another, The Entrance into the Promised Land. Paracelsus also should be read before all among elder writers, and, among other treatises, his Chemical Pathway, or the Manual of Paracelsus, which contains all the mysteries of demonstrative physics and the most arcane Kabbalah. This rare and unique manuscript work exists only in the Vatican Library, but Sendivogius had the good fortune to take a copy of it, which has helped in the illumination of the sages of our order. Secondly, Raymond Lully must be read, and his Vade Mecum above all, his dialogue called the Tree of Life, his testament, and his codicil. There must, however, be a certain precaution exercised in respect to the two last, because, like those of Geber, and also of Arnold de Villanova, they abound in false recipes and futile fictions, which seem to have been inserted with the object of more effectually disguising the truth from the ignorant. In the third place, the Turba Philosophorum which is a collection of ancient authors, contains much that is materially good, though there is much also which is valueless. Among mediaeval writers Zachary, Trevisan, Roger Bacon, and a certain anonymous author, whose book is entitled The Philosophers, should be held especially high in the estimation of the student. Among moderns the most worthy to be prized are John Fabricius, Francois de Nation, and Jean D'Espagnet, who wrote Physics Restored, though, to say the truth, he has imported some false precepts and fallacious opinions into his treatise.

Q. When may the Philosopher venture to undertake the work?

A. When he is, theoretically, able to extract, by means of a crude spirit, a digested spirit out of a body in dissolution, which digested spirit he must again rejoin to the vital oil.

Q. Explain me this theory in a clearer manner.

A. It may be demonstrated more completely in the actual process; the great experiment may be undertaken when the Philosopher, by the medium of a vegetable menstruurn, united to a mineral menstruum, is qualified to dissolve a third essential menstruum, with which menstruums united he must wash the earth, and then exalt it into a celestial quintessence, to compose the sulphureous thunderbolt, which instantaneously penetrates substances and destroys their excrements.

Q. Have those persons a proper acquaintance with Nature who pretend to make use of vulgar gold for seed, and of vulgar mercury for the dissolvent, or the earth in which it should be sown?

A. Assuredly not, because neither the one nor the other possesses the external agent--gold, because it has been deprived of it by decoction, and mercury because it has never had it.

Q. In seeking this auriferous seed elsewhere than in gold itself, is there no danger of producing a species of monster, since one appears to be departing from Nature?

A. It is undoubtedly true that in gold is contained the auriferous seed, and that in a more perfect condition than it is found in any other body; but this does not force us to make use of vulgar gold, for such a seed is equally found in each of the other metals, and is nothing else but that fixed grain which Nature has infused in the first congelation of mercury, all metals having one origin and a common substance, as will be ultimately unveiled to those who become worthy of receiving it by application and assiduous study.

Q. What follows from this doctrine?

A. It follows that, although the seed is more perfect in gold, it may be extracted much more easily from another body than from gold itself, other bodies being more open, that is to say, less digested, and less restricted in their humidity.

Q. Give me an example taken from Nature.

A. Vulgar gold may be likened to a fruit which, having come to a perfect maturity, has been cut off from its tree, and though it contains a most perfect and well-digested seed, notwithstanding, should anyone set it in the ground, with a view to its multiplication, much time, trouble, and attention will be consumed in the development of its vegetative capabilities. On the other hand, if a cutting, or a root, be taken from the same tree, and similarly planted, in a short time, and with no trouble, it will spring up and produce much fruit.

Q. Is it necessary that an amateur of this science should understand the formation of metals in the bowels of the earth if he wishes to complete his work?

A. So indispensable is such a knowledge that should anyone fail, before all other studies, to apply himself to its attainment, and to imitate Nature point by point therein, he will never succeed in accomplishing anything but what is worthless.

Q. How, then, does Nature deposit metals in the bowels of the earth, and of what does she compose them?

A. Nature manufactures them all out of sulphur and mercury, and forms them by their double vapour.

Q. What do you mean by this double vapour, and how can metals be formed thereby?

A. In order to a complete understanding of this question, it must first be stated that mercurial vapour is united to sulphureous vapour in a cavernous place which contains a saline water, which serves as their matrix. Thus is formed, firstly, the Vitriol of Nature; secondly, by the commotion of the elements, there is developed out of this Vitriol of Nature a new vapour, which is neither mercurial nor sulphureous, yet is allied to both these natures, and this, passing through places to which the grease of sulphur adheres, is joined therewith, and out of their union a glutinous substance is produced, otherwise, a formless mass, which is permeated by the vapour that fills these cavernous places. By this vapour, acting through the sulphur it contains, are produced the perfect metals, provided that the vapour and the locality are pure. If the locality and the vapour are impure, imperfect metals result. The terms perfection and imperfection have reference to various degrees of concoction.

Q. What is contained in this vapour?

A. A spirit of light and a spirit of fire, of the nature of the celestial bodies, which properly should be considered as the form of the universe.

Q. What does this vapour represent?

A. This vapour, thus impregnated by the universal spirit, represents, in a fairly complete way, the original Chaos, which contained all that was required for the original creation, that is, universal matter and universal form.

Q. And one cannot, notwithstanding, make use of vulgar mercury in the process?

A. No, because vulgar mercury, as already made plain, is devoid of external agent.

Q. Whence comes it that common mercury is without its external agent?

A. Because in the exaltation of the double vapour, the commotion has been so great and searching, that the spirit, or agent, has evaporated, as occurs, with very close similarity, in the fusion of metals. The result is that the unique mercurial part is deprived of its masculine or sulphureous agent, and consequently can never be transmuted into gold by Nature.

Q. How many species of gold are distinguished by the Philosophers?

A. Three sorts :--Astral Gold, Elementary Gold, and Vulgar Gold.

Q. What is astral gold?

A. Astral Gold has its centre in the sun, which communicates it by its rays to all inferior beings. It is an igneous substance, which receives a continual emanation of solar corpuscles that penetrate all things sentient, vegetable, and mineral.

Q. What do you refer to under the term Elementary Gold?

A. This is the most pure and fixed portion of the elements, and of all that is composed of them. All sublunary beings included in the three kingdoms contain in their inmost centre a precious grain of this elementary gold.

Q. Give me some description of Vulgar Gold?

A. It is the most beautiful metal of our acquaintance, the best that Nature can produce, as perfect as it is unalterable in itself.

Q. Of what species of gold is the Stone of the Philosophers?

A. It is of the second species, as being the most pure portion of all the metallic elements after its purification, when it is termed living philosophical gold. A perfect equilibrium and equality of the four elements enter into the Physical Stone, and four things are indispensable for the accomplishment of the work, namely, composition, allocation, mixture, and union, which, once performed according to the rules of art, will beget the lawful Son of the Sun, and the Phoenix which eternally rises out of its own ashes.

Q. What is actually the living gold of the Philosophers?

A. It is exclusively the fire of Mercury, or that igneous virtue, contained in the radical moisture, to which it has already communicated the fixity and the nature of the sulphur, whence it has emanated, the mercurial character of the whole substance of philosophical sulphur permitting it to be alternatively termed mercury.

Q. What other name is also given by the Philosophers to their living gold?

A. They also term it their living sulphur, and their true fire; they recognize its existence in all bodies, and there is nothing that can subsist without it.

Q. Where must we look for our living gold, our living sulphur, and our true fire?

A. In the house of Mercury.

Q. By what is this fire nourished?

A. By the air.

Q. Give me a comparative illustration of the power of this fire?

A. To exemplify the attraction of this interior fire, there is no better comparison than that which is derived from the thunderbolt, which originally is simply a dry, terrestrial exhalation, united to a humid vapour. By exaltation, and by assuming the igneous nature, it acts on the humidity which is inherent to it; this it attracts to itself, transmutes it into its own nature, and then rapidly precipitates itself to the earth, where it is attracted by a fixed nature which is like unto its own.

Q. What should be done by the Philosopher after he has extracted his Mercury?

A. He should develop it from potentiality into activity.

Q. Cannot Nature perform this of herself?

A. No; because she stops short after the first sublimation, and out of the matter which is thus disposed do the metals engender.

Q. What do the Philosophers understand by their gold and silver?

A. The Philosophers apply to their Sulphur the name of Gold, and to their Mercury the name of Silver.

Q. Whence are they derived?

A. I have already stated that they are derived from a homogeneous body wherein they are found in great abundance, whence also Philosophers know how to extract both by an admirable, and entirely philosophical, process.

Q. When this operation has been duly performed, to what other point of the practice must they next apply themselves?

A. To the confection of the philosophical amalgam, which must be done with great care, but can only be accomplished after the preparation and sublimation of the Mercury.

Q. When should your matter be combined with the living gold?

A. During the period of amalgamation only, that is to say, Sulphur is introduced into it by means of the amalgamation, and thenceforth there is one substance; the process is shortened by the addition of Sulphur, while the tincture at the same time is augmented.

Q. What is contained in the centre of the radical moisture ?
A. It contains and conceals Sulphur, which is covered with a hard rind.
Q. What must be done to apply it to the Great Work?
A. It must be drawn, out of its bonds with consummate skill, and by the method of putrefaction.
Q. Does Nature, in her work in the mines, possess a menstruum which is adapted to the dissolution and liberation of this sulphur?
A. No; because there is no local movement. Could Nature, unassisted, dissolve, putrefy, and purify the metallic body, she would herself provide us with !he Physical Stone, which is Sulphur exalted and increased in virtue.
Q. Can you elucidate this doctrine by an example?
A. By an enlargement of the previous comparison of a fruit, or a seed, which, in the first place, is put into the earth for its solution, and afterwards for its multiplication. Now, the Philosopher, who is in a position to discern what is good seed, extracts it from its centre, consigns it to its proper earth, when it has been well cured and prepared, and therein he rarefies it in such a manner that its prolific virtue is increased and indefinitely multiplied.
Q. In what does the whole secret of the seed consist ?
A. In the true knowledge of its proper earth.
Q. What do you understand by the seed in the work Of the Philosophers ?
A. I understand the interior heat, or the specific spirit, which is enclosed in the humid radical, which, in other words, is the middle substance of living silver, the proper sperm of metals, which contains its own seed.
Q. How do you set free the sulphur from its bonds?
A. By putrefaction.
Q. What is the earth of minerals ?
A. It is their proper menstruum.
Q. What pains must be taken by the Philosopher to extract that part which he requires?
A. He must take great pains to eliminate the fetid vapours and impure sulphurs, after which the seed must be injected.
Q. By what indication may the Artist be assured that he is in the right road at the beginning of his work?
A. When he finds that the dissolvent and the thing dissolved are converted into one form and one matter at the period of dissolution.

Q. How many solutions do you count in the Philosophic Work?
A. There are three. The first solution is that which reduces the crude and metallic body into its elements of sulphur and of living silver; the second is that of the physical body, and the third is the solution of the mineral earth.
Q. How is the metallic body reduced by the first solution into mercury, and then into sulphur?
A. By the secret artificial fire, which is the Burning Star.
Q. How is this operation performed?
A. By extracting from the subject, in the first place, the mercury or vapour of the elements, and, after purification, by using it to liberate the sulphur from its bonds, by corruption, of which blackness is the indication.
Q. How is the second solution performed?
A. When the physical body is resolved into the two substances previously mentioned, and has acquired the celestial nature.
Q. What is the name which is applied by Philosophers to the Matter during this period?
A, It is called their Physical Chaos, and it is, in fact, the true First Matter, a name which can hardly be applied before the conjunction of the male--which is sulphur--with the female--which is silver.
Q. To what does the third solution refer?
A. It is the humectation of the mineral earth and it is closely bound up with multiplication.
Q. What fire must be made use of in our work?
A. That fire which is used by Nature.
Q. What is the potency of this fire?
A. It dissolves everything that is in the world, because it is the principle of all dissolution and corruption.
Q. Why is it also termed Mercury?
A. Because it is in its nature aerial, and a most subtle vapour, which partakes at the same time of sulphur, whence it has contracted some contamination.
Q. Where is this fire concealed?
A. It is concealed in the subject of art.
Q. Who is it that is familiar with, and can produce, this fire?
A. It is known to the wise, who can both produce it and purify it.
Q. What is the essential potency and characteristic of this fire?
A. It is excessively dry, and is continually in motion; it seeks only to disintegrate and to educe things from potentiality into actuality;

it is that, in a word, which coming upon solid places in mines, circulates in a vaporous form upon the matter, and dissolves it.
Q. How may this fire be most easily distinguished?
A. By the sulphureous excrements in which it is enveloped, and by the saline environment with which it is clothed.
Q. What must be added to this fire so as to accentuate its capacity for incineration in the feminine species?
A. On account of its extreme dryness it requires to be moistened.
Q. How many philosophical fires do you enumerate?
A. There are in all three--the natural, the unnatural, and the contra-natural.
Q. Explain to me these three species of fires.
A. The natural fire is the masculine fire, or the chief agent; the unnatural is the feminine, which is the dissolvent of Nature, nourishing a white smoke, and assuming that form. This smoke is quickly dissipated, unless much care be exercised, and it is almost incombustible, though by philosophical sublimation it becomes corporeal and resplendent. The contra-natural fire is that which disintegrates compounds and has the power to unbind what has' been bound very closely by Nature.
Q. Where is our matter to be found?
A. It is to be found everywhere, but it must specially be sought in metallic nature, where it is more easily available than elsewhere.
Q. What kind must be preferred before all others?
A. The most mature, the most appropriate, and the easiest; but care, before all things, must be taken that the metallic essence shall be present, not only potentially but in actuality, and that there is, moreover, a metallic splendour.
Q. Is everything contained in this subject?
A. Yes; but Nature, at the same time, must be assisted, so that the work may be perfected and hastened, and this by the means which are familiar to the higher grades of experiment.
Q. Is this subject exceedingly precious?
A. It is vile, and originally is without native elegance; should anyone say that it is saleable, it is the species to which they refer, but, fundamentally, it is not saleable, because it is useful in our work alone.
Q. What does our Matter contain?
A. It contains Salt, Sulphur, and Mercury.
Q. What operation is it most important to be able to perform?
A. The successive extraction of the Salt, Sulphur, and Mercury.

Q. How is that done?
A. By sole and perfect sublimation.
Q. What is in the first place extracted?
A. Mercury in the form of a white smoke.
Q. What follows?
A. Igneous water, or Sulphur.
Q. What then?
A. Dissolution with purified salt, in the first place volatilising that which is fixed, and afterwards fixing that which is volatile into a precious earth, which is the Vase of the Philosophers, and is wholly perfect.
Q. When must the Philosopher begin his enterprise?
A. At the moment of daybreak, for his energy must never be relaxed.
Q. When may he take his rest?
A. When the work has come to its perfection.
Q. At what hour is the end of the work?
A. High noon, that is to say, the moment when the Sun is in its fullest power, and the Son of the Day-Star in its most brilliant splendour.
Q. What is the pass-word of Magnesia?
A. You know whether I can or should answer:--I reserve my speech.
Q. Give me the greeting of the Philosophers.
A. Begin ; I will reply to you.
Q. Are you an apprentice Philosopher?
A. My friends, and the wise, know me.
Q. What is the age of a Philosopher?
A. From the moment of his researches to that of his discoveries, the Philosopher does not age.

www.ingramcontent.com/pod-product-compliance
Lightning Source LLC
Chambersburg PA
CBHW072147160426
43197CB00012B/2276